COMPASSION
IN
ACTION

May 16 1992

To dearest Tilak

Vandana
Apurva

Also by Ram Dass

BE HERE NOW (1971)
THE ONLY DANCE THERE IS (1974)
GRIST FOR THE MILL (with Stephen Levine, 1977)
JOURNEY OF AWAKENING (1978)
MIRACLE OF LOVE (1979)
HOW CAN I HELP? (with Paul Gorman, 1985)

COMPASSION IN ACTION

Setting Out on the Path of Service

Ram Dass

AND

Mirabai Bush

BELL TOWER/NEW YORK

Published by Bell Tower, an imprint of Harmony Books, a division of Crown Publishers, Inc., 201 East 50th Street, New York, New York 10022. Member of the Crown Publishing Group.

Harmony, Bell Tower, and colophon are trademarks of Crown Publishers, Inc.

Manufactured in the United States of America

Library of Congress Cataloging-in-Publication Data

Ram Dass.
    Compassion in action : setting out on the path of service / Ram Dass and Mirabai Bush.—1st ed.
        p.   cm.
    1. Altruism.   2. Voluntarism.   3. Spiritual life.   4. Ram Dass.   I. Bush, Mirabai, 1939–   .   II. Title.
    BF637.H4R35   1992
    158'.3—dc20   91-20223
                                                            CIP

ISBN 0-517-57635-X

10 9 8 7 6 5 4 3 2 1

First Edition

For Neem Karoli Baba
who is *compassion in action*

Contents

Acknowledgments

In a book celebrating the interconnection of all life in all times and places, it is hard to know where to start the acknowledgments and where to stop. But there are a few people who contributed so directly to these pages that we want to mention them here.

The family that is Seva Foundation infused the book with its spirit. Through their lives and their work, many of our friends in Seva suggested the themes that the book develops, and many passionate discussions among us opened up the central questions asked here. Paul Gorman, coauthor with Ram Dass of *How Can I Help?*, was the book's godfather, blessing it with encouragement, advice, and humor. Dr. T. Stephen Jones of the Centers for Disease Control provided the latest information on AIDS. Sharon Salzberg of Insight Meditation Society, with whom we have done the Buddhist *metta* meditation for twenty years, shared her insight into the qualities of loving-kindness, compassion, and generosity.

Coming to know the Mayan people of Guatemala, where Seva is working in grass-roots development, has deepened our appreciation of the power of community and the possibility of change in the face of incredible odds. We thank Jahanara Romney for first taking us there; Sunanda Markus, Frank Taylor, and Carsta Neuenroth for bringing their hearts and minds so fully to the work; and Don Vicente Gabriel for embodying the spirit of the *campesino*.

The many people interviewed for the book helped form the ideas and inspired us with their frontline embodiment of compassionate action. Although not everyone is mentioned by name in the text, every one contributed something; among those who helped in special ways not mentioned elsewhere were Ravi Khanna, Steve Schwartz, Nan Seamans, Willie Brown, Johnnie May Baylis, Frieda Garcia, Marjorie Bayes, and Nancy Schwoyer.

Loving friends and fierce critics—Owen Bush, Rayner Ramirez, Erik Lerner, Dan and Tara Goleman, Jai Lakshman, Sunanda Markus, Peter Heil, Joseph Goldstein, Larry Brilliant, and Kedar Harris—all read parts of the book in early stages and gave honest responses that resulted in helpful revision. Marlene Roeder typed, transcribed, faxed, Fed-Exed, and was always there when we needed her.

And our deepest thanks to E. J. Lynch, who loved us, fed us, and shared his comforting common sense. And to Toinette Lippe, our editor, who encouraged us throughout this project, kept our shoulders to the wheel, and helped us wrap what at times looked like two separate books into a unified whole.

Preface

This book is for those of us who feel called to reduce the suffering that surrounds us on the planet and who also feel that the deepest responsibility of each of us is to become more fully who we are, to live closer to the truth. It is part of a tradition that says that the two happen simultaneously, that each nourishes the other. It is about the interdependence of social and spiritual development, in the sense of de-enveloping, or uncovering and revealing the truth within suffering, the world, and ourselves.

In 1985, Ram Dass and Paul Gorman published *How Can I Help?*, which explored "the nature of conscious service and the challenges posed by the present conditions." That book examined what sustains us in our work, how attachment to concepts such as giver and receiver keeps us in "helping prison," and how our service is involved in the process of healing in the broadest sense. The incredible response it evoked led to another question—how do we *begin* to act compassionately for change? What are the first steps toward the conscious relief of suffering? Especially, how do we begin those actions for change that may not happen naturally and spontaneously, the kind that stretch the arm's reach, may take thought and effort to begin, and may involve people we don't already know but for whom our hearts are hurting.

We are searching for a way of acting for social change in the world that is compatible with, in fact contributes to, psychological, intellectual, and spiritual growth, and acknowledges that, as Gandhi said, our life is our message. We are exploring what the Dalai Lama calls "selfish altruism": compassionate action is not done *for* others—it is done *with* others, *for* ourselves, because we can no longer avoid it. It helps fulfill our lives.

As we explored the issues that arose, we thought that an autobiographical reflection by Ram Dass might provide a familiar entrance into what is for many of us a new arena. We recognized, of course, that each of our lives unfolds in its own way, but we felt that one person's journey could remind others that the development of compassionate action is a continual process, one of discovering ever new questions rather than answers. This narrative is followed by a reflection on the nature of service as a spiritual practice, "the path of action." To help that process begin, to get us actually onto the road, we have added some "first steps": thoughts and encouragement for entering the world of service, stories and quotations from many people already there, and resources and suggestions on where to begin.

Both working in the world and preparing this book have reminded us once again that words are barely fingers pointing at the moon, that all concepts hide the truth, and that the map is not the territory. But limited as these words are, may they inspire us to walk the path, learn the lessons, and work together with love.

CALLED
BY
COMPASSION

Ram Dass and Mirabai Bush

Compassion in action is paradoxical and mysterious. It is absolute yet continually changing. It accepts that everything is happening exactly as it should, and it works with a full-hearted commitment to change. It sets goals but knows that the process is all there is. It is joyful in the midst of suffering and hopeful in the face of overwhelming odds. It is simple in a world of complexity and confusion. It is done for others, but it nurtures the self. It shields in order to be strong. It intends to eliminate suffering, knowing that suffering is limitless. It is action arising from emptiness.

When we look at the vast sadness and suffering in the world, we often experience intense pain in our hearts. The suffering so often seems cruel, unnecessary, and unjustified—reflecting a heartless universe. The human greed and fear that are causing much of the suffering seem out of control. But when our hearts open in the midst of this, we want to help. This is the experience of compassion.

Compassion is the tender opening of our hearts to pain and suffering. When compassion arises in us, we see and acknowledge what we often push away—the parts of life that cause us sadness, anger, or outrage. The powerful awakening of our own compassion can tune us not just to the nurturing and sustaining forces of the world but to the oppressive and destructive ones as well. When we open to these directly and become familiar with them, instead of avoiding them as we often do, we are more likely to hear ways to respond with love and support to relieve the suffering. When the pain is our own, we want to end it. If we can't do this by ourselves, we long for help. When it is not our cry, but someone else's, compassion allows us to feel it as our own, to feel the same longing, to hear our hearts calling us to help. The Dalai Lama has said, "Love and compassion are necessities, not luxuries. Without them, humanity cannot survive. With them, we can make a joint effort to solve the problems of the whole of humankind."

Acting with compassion is not doing good because we think we ought to. It is being drawn to action by heartfelt passion. It is giving ourselves into what we are doing, being present in the moment—no matter how difficult, sad, or even boring it feels, no matter how much it demands. It is acting from our deepest understanding of what life is, listening intently for the skillful means in each situation, and not compromising the truth. It is working with others in a selfless way, in a spirit of mutual respect.

Compassion is the basis of all truthful relationship: it means being present with love—for ourselves and for all life, including animals, fish, birds, and trees. Compassion is bringing our deepest truth into our actions, no matter how much the world seems to resist, because that is ultimately what we have to give this world and one another.

Suffering exists, pain exists, cruelty and injustice exist. We can't deny that, and we can't eliminate it all no matter how hard we try. What we can do is bring truth and loving-kindness into each situation in which we find ourselves. We can use suffering as an opportunity for expressing love. When others are suffering, we can't always make them happy, no matter how much we want to, but we can create an environment in which wholesome choices are more likely, and we can support one another in our attempts toward more fulfilling lives. We can't "fix" one another's lives, but we can help one another gain insight and skill so that we all have more control over our lives, so that we are not more dependent but are more free. What we can give one another is support—from tender care to the temporary fulfillment of basic human needs.

Life on earth, diverse and wonderful, includes our human community of interconnected people, all of us carrying the spirit, all of us with the ability to respond effectively to our own problems if we have the proper resources. For complex reasons, many of us do not have those resources now and need the support and help of others to shift the balance. There are ways for each of us to participate in this shift. This book is an exploration of some of those ways.

Compassion begins with ourselves. When we are kind and caring toward ourselves, we are nurturing our spiritual growth and cultivating compassion for others. Gandhi, whose life was committed to the relief of suffering for others, understood this; he said, "I believe in the essential unity of all people and for that matter, of all that lives. Therefore, I believe that if one person gains spiritually, the whole world gains, and if one person falls, the whole world falls to that extent." What we have to give is who we are; when we are kind and forgiving toward ourselves, we are more relaxed and happy and better able to be loving toward others. Compassionate action is a path on which we grow in awareness and insight. As we grow, we become purer instruments for change. We become hollow reeds for the healing music of life.

We all frequently act with compassion toward people familiar to us and the ground we live on; we teach our children, listen to our friends, tend our gardens. This book offers "first steps" toward another kind of compassionate action, the kind we may need help in discovering, the kind that extends further than our immediate arms' reach. It explores possibilities for acting with love, care, truth, and passion toward those who are calling from a distance.

They may be calling because of AIDS, hunger, or the denial of their human rights, but their voices are reaching us. Our individual caring responses do not mean that public commitment is not also needed; even if every one of us taught someone to read, our schools would still need programs to prevent and correct illiteracy. But when we hear the cry, in order to continue to live honestly with ourselves and others, we want to respond. And that response may bring some of us closer together and eliminate a part of the world's pain. The rest of this book has been written to help us in the process.

FINDING MY CARING HEART

Ram Dass

Introduction

A Buddhist monk once said: "He who clings to the void and neglects compassion does not reach the highest stage. But he who practices only compassion does not gain release from the toils of existence. He however who is strong in the practice of both, remains neither in samsara nor in nirvana."

Over time I have come to appreciate the relationship between emptiness and compassion. Lines in the mystic literature, such as "Out of emptiness arises compassion," suggest this link. Here the void means the silence that exists within sound, the deepest spiritual roots of life itself. Compassion refers to the arising in the heart of the desire to relieve the suffering of all beings. At its most evolved form, compassionate action does not arise solely out of personal desire. Rather, in bodhisattvalike fashion, it arises from a desire created by the collective suffering of all beings.

In the first part of this book, I'd like to share with you, in a very personal way, what I have learned about compassion. I realize, of course, that each of us has our own particular lessons to learn and that there are many different ways of learning them. But while the specifics of our journeys may not be of much use to other people, I have found that when we share them honestly with one another, they can strengthen our faith.

There are two questions I am informally addressing here. First, what are the roots of my own caring action? The other question I have reflected about is what we can actually do for one another. What have we to offer one another to alleviate suffering?

Regarding the first question, the way in which I serve others has changed over time. At first there was self-consciousness, long-suffering, righteous indignation, power preoccupation, pride, burnout, and the like. While my actions might have looked compassionate or caring to others, the inside story was quite another matter. But, over time, some of the ego's reasons, fears, and complaints about serving have lost much of their power. Now I can see the possibility that appropriate serving to relieve the suffering of other beings could become simply what I do. Like breathing. It's nothing special.

The second question was, What have we to offer one another to alleviate suffering? It's obvious that a hungry belly we can fill with food, a frightened child we can comfort, a person blind with cataract we can help to see again, a homeless person we can assist in finding affordable housing, and a destitute farmer we can provide with seeds, tools, and water for growing food. We can bear witness to governments' acts of inhumanity toward their citizens and speak out, and we can console the sick and lonely, the dying, and the grieving.

But there is more that we can do even as we are performing these caring acts. We can honor the profound ancient wisdom that reminds us that one of the roots of suffering lies deep within our own minds. By remembering that and learning to work with these root causes within ourselves, even as we attempt to help others, we find that our own inner work becomes part of our offering to others.

The late Kalu Rinpoche, an extraordinary Tibetan Buddhist lama, once said to me: "You have only three things to do in this lifetime. Honor your guru. Deepen your emptiness. Deepen your compassion." That simple prescription embraces so much of what my life has become. Spiritual practice has not only kept alive my relationship to my guru, Neem Karoli Baba, who is my inner guide, but has also allowed me to taste the emptiness that lies behind all form. And my life in the world has taught me about compassion.

Here, then, is the story of one person's continuing attempt to integrate spirit into service.

The Early Years

It was not until I was thirty years old, in 1961, that some qualities of true compassion began to awaken in me, or, perhaps I should say, to reawaken. Up until then I had felt pity, sympathy, and undoubtedly guilt for the suffering of others. I had even wanted to do something about it and, indeed, had done so. But the motivation for my actions was never rooted in what I could call real compassion toward others.

I was born into a culture of separateness. The first years of life were basically "somebody" training. I was learning how to be somebody . . . I hoped somebody special or important but, at the very least, somebody. The "somebody" training was so successful that I soon lived almost exclusively in my separate ego. Everything and everybody was seen through the lenses of ego and its instruments:

desires, attitudes, and concepts. Other people were perceived as either gratifying my desires or not; loving me or not; enhancing my social psychological power or not; providing security or not. I assumed that the alienation I felt was experienced by everybody. I even taught psychology from that frame of reference. I didn't realize that what I had gained in personal power had been acquired at the expense of losing my heart connection with other people. I was imprisoned in my separateness.

Of course we all have to learn to inhabit our individuality. But, in doing that, we do not need to lose our sense of identity with others. It is only when that identity with others survives the socialization process that we can act out of genuine compassion. What I lost in my self-preoccupation as a child, I would find again only thirty years later.

As I look back on family life with Dad and Mother and my two older brothers, I remember fun and play and love and happiness, but I more frequently remember fighting, sternness, picking on one another, anger, hurt, loneliness, and frustration. Most of all, what I recall from my early years is our excessive preoccupation with our own personas, our own somebodyness. We were five individuals, each self-consciously separate from the others. The fact that we were a "family" was never uppermost in our collective consciousness.

When I look at the pictures of myself, I see a cheerful, bright, secure child. I'm told that I was. But what is on the outside of the package does not necessarily correspond to what is on the inside. What I remember of my early years is my obsession with the approval and love of "important people," i.e., the people in my life to whom I gave power.

On reflection, I see that this need for approval was the motivation for most of my "kindly" acts in my first thirty years. I would more or less figure out what kind of a person I needed to be to win approval, and that was who I would become. If you wanted "caring," I was caring.

While, as a psychologist, I had many theories about how I had gotten to be this way, for many years I had no emotional memories of the first four or five years of my life, when, I assumed, these patterns had been laid down. The veil that covered that period seemed to be so thick that it resisted years of psychoanalysis, psychedelics, and meditation. Not until 1981 did I have an experience that broke through the barrier and reawakened a direct emotional memory that rent the veil and gave me access to that shadowy past.

It happened in Hawaii, and the story starts when my plane landed at the Hilo airport on the "big island" of Hawaii and I looked around for my hosts. I was on a speaking tour leading workshops on Oahu, Maui, and Kauai. I had never visited the big island, the island of Hawaii itself, so I decided to sandwich in a visit in response to a nonincome-generating invitation: "We are a group living together and meditating together up in the hills of the island of Hawaii, and we invite you to visit with us."

A young couple and an older man gathered up me and my baggage, and we all climbed into the wide front seat of a huge Bronco truck and headed for the old coffee plantation where they lived. When I first met them, I was Ram Dass, that charismatic, charming, spiritual friend identity that I was used to sliding into with considerable alacrity. A few minutes into the trip I realized that they were silent, not offering me the reactive wherewithal to generate more Ram Dass–ness. They were strange, very strange, though I didn't yet realize how much so.

After an hour of driving and climbing, we arrived at the plantation. I rested for a while, then joined the older man in his quarters. We watched a magnificent sunset together, and we were brought a big platter of freshly cut tropical fruit for supper.

Then he said, "I think it's time to meet the others." He drew a curtain that separated his room from the rest of the building, and I found myself looking at about thirty people who had all been sitting there quietly and undetected. It was arranged so that everyone was facing me and everyone seemed to be waiting for me to speak.

So I started to speak—to tell stories, to do whatever it is I do. After a few minutes, a fellow near the back of the room raised his hand. When I recognized him, he said, "Ram Dass, your book *Be Here Now* was very helpful. Why aren't you like your book?" His remark was like a bucket of iced water thrown in my face. The innuendo did not escape me, and I could feel my defensive hackles rising. Then a girl in another part of the room spoke up: "I don't feel much heart in what you are saying." Others spoke up in the same vein, and I began to freak. They all began to look like enemies to me, and I started to attack. I implied that I was fine and openhearted, and that it was they who were screwed up.

This horror show went on from about nine thirty in the evening until midnight, with one after another criticizing me. Finally the doctor, who had been mostly quiet throughout the evening, said, "I think we've gone about as far as we can go tonight. Why don't we start around seven thirty in the morning?" Everyone dispersed silently, and I was left alone to return to my sleeping space.

What the hell was this all about? I was in real pain. I had come expecting to share an evening with a gentle meditation group. So much for expectations. And now, in the dark, I couldn't escape from this remote coffee plantation. I had told them originally that I could stay until late morning of the coming day. Who were they? What did they want of me? As I lay in bed looking out at the stars, I quieted down, and I realized that they were right—that I was still a phony, that I had been covering and defending my vulnerability all evening. The feelings of humiliation and embarrassment were intense.

The next morning at seven thirty, when we gathered, I opened by telling them of my insights of the previous night. They had been right in their accusations, I told them, and, though I didn't particularly like them, I wanted to ask for their help. When I've told this story since the event, my listeners often have had a hard time understanding how I could have surrendered to this coercive scene the way I did. Was it some masochistic streak in me, or such a powerful need to be loved, or what?

I don't really know for sure, but it seems to me that at moments like that, my desire to grow and awaken and become free is so strong that I move toward the situation, just or unjust as it may be. I guess my hope is that through working with what is so clearly traumatic I may ferret out some of the tenacious ego traits lurking in the more devious hiding places in my psyche.

So I threw myself on their mercy, and they told me to keep talking. And I talked and confessed all of my shame, my fears, my misery. I told them what a good boy I had always been and how one of my brothers had become mentally disturbed and in effect disowned the family. At this point, the doctor suggested that perhaps my brother was the only one of us kids who had retained any power, and that I, in my zeal to be loved, out of my feeling that I was unlovable, had sold out, had given my power away.

All at once I am no longer in the Hawaiian hills. I am back in my childhood bedroom, in my crib, the sun streaming in through the bars. I am having a temper tantrum. I am screaming and feeling my own deepest pain and power. The doctor and the group lay me down. They make my hands into fists, and they surround me, their hands on my now prone body. They are encouraging me to make sounds. I am groaning in agony, screaming with rage. I am alive. The feeling is immensely sensual.

I feel/see in my mind's eye my mother standing over my crib, demanding I stop, holding my arms and looking at this male child, this part of herself that she cannot control, looking with scorn and rejection. I am fighting her with all my power, but she gives me no quarter. She just holds my arms and looks at me coldly. It is that look that turns the tide, because, if I lose her love, I lose everything. I feel myself flicker, then I am overcome with a paroxysm of defeat and I have relinquished my power. It is as simple as that.

As I quieted down and came back into the room with those thirty people in Hawaii, I realized that this memory, so long lost from view in the dark abyss of my mind, was true. And with its uncovering I felt a new wholeness in my being, as if a part of me that was dead had come back to life. It took thirty of them, and this contrived social situation and imprisonment, to do what years of analysis, drugs, and meditation had been unable to do. I still didn't like these people and felt they had no right to do what they did to me, yet I was thankful to them for this reprieve from the early, almost preconceptual, personality calcification in which I had been frozen.

In time other memories flooded back, and I realized that I had come away from that very early traumatic experience feeling that I had power only when my mother gave it to me. That and her often intensely intimate loving quality combined to focus my energies on pleasing the power figures around me; first, my mother and father, later all their surrogates. During the early years, my mother, who was a good woman, was an important role model for me. She was always "doing" for somebody else, putting others' needs ahead of her own. However, I won her love not by doing for others but by letting her do for me. She infantilized me as her "baby," especially after I barely survived two bouts of pneumonia when I was eight. I don't remember her praising me for "doing" for others, though I recall many times when I imitated her doing for others as a way of making myself feel like a good boy.

I physically pushed away my pubescence for as long as possible in order to remain a needy child and thus keep her close. When, with the help of thyroid medicine, I finally entered adolescence, I recall returning from board- ing school, hugging her a moment too long, and feeling sexual excitement. She pushed me away, red-faced, and established the sanctity of the incest taboo by leading me to the kitchen for milk and fresh, hot brownies.

This intense love for my mother continued to be very deep, even though I tried to push her away as I entered adulthood. I stood by helplessly for ten years watching her suffer greatly with a blood condition from which she finally died. This experience drove me even more deeply into my intellectual defenses as a way of distancing my- self from others' pain, and also their love. I couldn't risk another relationship that would entail such heartbreak and loss of control.

I focus at such length on these early experiences with my mother because in them lie the roots of my ability, or rather my inability, to feel an identity with others' suf- fering. My needs for power and reassurance, just to exist, were too strong to leave space for real caring. And, had I opened my heart to others, my vulnerability and impo- tence would have overwhelmed me. So I hid in my in- tellect to protect my heart. From these early experiences with my mother also came the idea that serving others involves long-suffering self-sacrifice, which, of course, is a way of controlling others.

Throughout my childhood and well into my adolescence, there were other experiences that undoubtedly fed, if not at the time then later, into my emerging ground of compassion. For example, I was bedridden for a part of each summer with skin troubles—poison ivy, oak, and such. I'm sure those frustrating months and other situations like them affected my feelings toward people who are confined because of physical illness. At the time, the suffering seemed grossly unfair and all but unbearable. In retrospect, I am no longer sure whether those summers in my room, when I heard everyone else outside playing, were a curse or a grace. Undoubtedly, they were both. They were a curse to that young boy but grace to the man who was to be.

Another episode stands out and undoubtedly deepened my ability to emphathize with such kinds of suffering. When I was sixteen years old at boarding school, I was caught in a nude wrestling episode with another boy. There were clear sexual overtones, and the upperclassmen who had spied on us through a hole in the closet wall lost no time in spreading the story throughout the school. Immediately I found the two of us ostracized. If I walked into a dorm room, conversation would stop until I left. This went on for almost a year. I didn't feel comfortable telling my parents. The faculty didn't seem to be able to handle the incident any better than the students. So I just went inside myself. It was only when a few popular boys risked social ostracism by befriending me that my ordeal of isolation ended. There was no time during that period or in the fifteen years immediately following that I ever congratulated myself on my good fortune at having had such an experience. But, in the last thirty years, I have come to see quite clearly how it affected me. It made me much more empathetic toward people outside the system. And the turning-inward, coerced though it was, proved a catalyst to help me find a place in myself where I could stand even in the absence of social support. It was this sense of connection to inner truth that gave me such strength when I was ostracized from academia and fired from Harvard for my psychedelic research.

My father, though more emotionally distant than my mother, played an important role in the formation of my attitude to the suffering of others. My association with Dad lasted over fifty-five years, until his death in 1987, so I find great value in studying our relationship because it passed through many stages as both he and I changed.

In my early years, up until the midsixties when I was already in my thirties, Dad was a successful and powerful man. First as a lawyer, then as a founding father of Brandeis University, and then as a railroad president, he was the strong father who provided well for his family. He was charitable and also a man very much focused upon his own career. I suspect that in the community he was more admired than liked.

I was the youngest of three boys, and, by the time I came along, his preoccupation with achievement had calmed down somewhat. But whatever my father and I did together, whether it was photography, fishing, or mowing the lawn, it was somehow cast in terms of achievement—his achievement.

By the time I was eight years old, Dad was already a recognized philanthropist and fund-raiser for the Jewish community. By 1942 he had become a national figure through his skill as an unsalaried fund-raiser and executive for the Joint Distribution Committee, a charity whose purpose was to relocate German Jewish children, whose lives had been shattered by the chaos of the Nazi "solution to the Jewish problem." He used his courtroom trial lawyer acumen to raise millions of dollars, mixing just the right amounts of horror, flattery, guilt awakening, humor, and cajoling to make giving feel good. I recall many evenings when Dad had worked the audience into such a frenzy of public giving that they were jostling one another to capture the microphone and announce their five-, ten-, twenty-five-, fifty-thousand-dollar gifts, or more, in honor of their new grandchild, wife, mother, or father.

While I was proud of Dad, I lived with him, or in close proximity to him, and was aware of how much his consciousness about this philanthropy was focused on his career. He equated success with knowing rich and powerful people, and the charities were the perfect vehicle to bring that opportunity about. I don't doubt that he had some real concern about the suffering European Jews; it's just that I can't ever remember our talking about it.

When one considers all the ways a community could choose to elevate and honor its members, charity is certainly one to be admired, and the Jews excel at it. But the motives for contributing—guilt, social shame or praise, and respect within the community—seem to leave something out. What was left out, or rather overshadowed, was compassion. The community rewarded not compassion but rather "giving." The two are very different.

One of Dad's lines about the German Jewish children that brought down the house was, "What would you do if it were your child? Well, I'll tell you that, if it were my child, I'd give every penny that I could beg, borrow . . .

or, yes, even steal." This was offered with a crack in the voice. Notice that he didn't say, These *are* your children. He said, If they *were* your children. . . . I recall later, when I was at prep school, winning second prize in a public speaking contest using his exact speech. And even though I and my audience were all teenagers, the line still worked.

These days, as I travel through the country fundraising for the Seva Foundation, I see my father in me. I too have skills as an orator, and I too raise money for the suffering of the world. Is it the same game he was playing, only masked in another way? Partly, I'm sure. As you will see, prior to 1961 the similarity might have been one of both form and motive, but after 1961 something had started to happen to me that affected my motives for doing and being. Up until that time I, as a psychologist, interpreted my life actions as a working-out of relationships with my parents. But, as with childhood games, there is a time to leave those motives behind. I am grateful that I was able to do that.

Part of my motivation for becoming a psychologist in the fifties was that I wanted to help people. But in my honest moments, which came out in therapy at the time, I acknowledged that the desire to help people arose out of a need to be needed, and an immense need for love and power. And by helping people seemingly selflessly, I got an abundant amount of all of these. However, though I needed to be loved, I was neither capable of loving nor really able to accept the love and admiration I received.

These preoccupations aroused in me a compelling fascination with personality dynamics, and this was undoubtedly a major determinant in my attraction to psychology as a career. And, of course, once I was active in that field, the fire of fascination fed upon itself. By the time I began teaching at Stanford, I assumed that a human being could be adequately described in terms of his or her personality dynamics: motivations, attitudes, cognitive models, et cetera. The psychoanalysis I was undergoing focused exclusively on transference and countertransference, and on psychosexual stages of ego development. And in the therapy I did, which was somehow remotely involved in helping others, I saw myself working with my "patients" for a motley variety of personal reasons: the need to feel powerful, righteous, loved; voyeuristic desires; problem-solving and status needs; the superiority awakened in conjunction with the feeling of pity for others; and the need for intimacy.

Because I had been trained to achieve as a way to receive approval, I ended up in research psychology, which, in the zeitgeist in which I took my training, was considered superior to clinical psychology. So it was through my intellect that I set out to "help." There was little heart in the matter, because we looked at people really as little more than sets of "ambulatory variables."

My psychological career flourished. I became a professor and researcher at Harvard University, serving also as a therapist at the University Health Services. While my interest in personality development and clinical pathology, as well as my role as a therapist, brought me into contact with issues of human suffering, my theories about the dynamics of it all kept me well insulated from any real sharing of the pain of others. Intellect was my Maginot Line of defense. This defense was overridden in only a very few instances, when I became so involved with clinical patients that my emotional attachments or righteous indignation threatened to debilitate me completely. Despite this inner turmoil and manipulation on my part, I think people at that time saw me as a compassionate person. On a superficial level I may have been fooling others, but I could not fool myself.

Most of the people I chose to associate with were either my elders, i.e., more powerful people to whom I was subservient, or people under me administratively, chronologically, experientially, or economically—people who needed my power. Later, when I had more space in my consciousness, I began to examine whether my strategy of either being around people who had more or less power than me or being alone was the best one. What about peers? I reflected upon why I acknowledged or spent time with so few peers. The obvious psychodynamic inferiority-superiority complex that had dogged me all of my life was at the root. But it was only in the sixties, when my personality no longer seemed to be the central core of my paradigm of reality, that I started to embrace the opportunity to work closely with peers.

People have asked me whether my Jewish lineage was part of the genesis of compassion. I went through bar mitzvah—the adolescent rite of passage—and we attended synagogue on the High Holy Days. At home, in the early days, we kept a kosher kitchen and only ate pork when we went out to Chinese restaurants. Dad performed *yahrzeit*—a ceremony remembering his parents on the anniversaries of their deaths—and was a member of the board of trustees of the synagogue, a suburban Conservative (not Orthodox) temple; and we fasted on the Day of Atonement. I remember a great deal of sentimentalizing, moralizing, and being aggrieved and resentful about our past sufferings, but I don't remember any living spirit connected with those practices or any awakening in me of an identity with the plight of others or concern for the suffering of humanity in general.

Many years later, in 1968, just after I returned from India for the first time, I had a conversation that shed some light on this. I was attending a ceremony for the unveiling of my mother's tombstone. The rabbi, a man I had never met, wearing a soft hat and sunglasses, was reading the prayers and saying a few words of condolence at the grave site. At that time I had a long beard and long hair, and wore many beads and Indian garb, an *ulfie* (which to the Western eye did look like a dress). But I also wore a yarmulke and read the prayers in Hebrew.

Perhaps it was the bizarreness of my appearance that caught the rabbi's attention, or perhaps he thought of me as my father's "fallen son" whom he should attempt to straighten out. Whatever! At the conclusion of the ceremony he came up to me, took me by the elbow, steered me away from the family, and in a professionally familiar way asked, "Well, what have you been up to?" I looked at him directly and asked, "Do you really want to know?" He said that he did, so, while we leaned on two tombstones, I told him a little about India, meeting my guru, miracles I had encountered, and the feelings of spirit that the experiences had awakened in me. As he listened, I noticed a visible change in his demeanor.

When I finally stopped, he said, as if speaking from far

away, "When I was studying for my final exams in the Bible, I took too many No Doz pills to stay awake. At one point, something happened. The book disappeared from my vision and I found myself living in the time of Isaac in Jerusalem. I was immersed in all of it. I was filled with rapture for hours."

I could hear in his voice a softness and reverence for that powerful experience. I recall saying to him after we had been silent together for some minutes, "What grace to have had such an experience. I imagine you have strengthened the faith of many of your congregation through sharing that story." My comment made him regain himself, and he stood straight, moving back toward the family, and answered me in his professional rabbinical voice, "Until today I have never shared that with a member of the congregation. Judaism is a folk religion and I am an interpreter of the law. Such a story has no relevance." As he said that, I recall a feeling of great sadness sweeping over me.

Despite the limits of my early religious training, I do find important roots in my Judaism. Not long ago, I was speaking at a university and a young rabbi asked me what my relationship was to Judaism. One of my friends, with irreverent reincarnational humor, has said that he is only Jewish on his parents' side. My friend's answer crossed my mind but did not seem appropriate, so I went inside and reflected quietly about it. After some time, I told the rabbi that I was not very drawn to the theology or practices. However, as a result of being a Jew, I felt that I had been imbued with three things: first, the sense that behind and within the multiplicity of forms there is One, seamless and radiant, and that loving that One, with all my being, is a path. Second, a love and respect for knowledge as a path to wisdom. And the third great gift I felt that I had received was an awareness of suffering and the compassion that arises with that awareness.

Turning Points

A critical turning point in my life occurred in the spring of 1961, but the seed had been planted the previous summer. I had flown my airplane to Mexico to meet with my colleague from the Harvard faculty, Timothy Leary. After I landed, Tim told me about a flight into his own mind that he had taken as a result of ingesting psilocybe mushrooms, which the Mexican *curanderos* call *teonanactyl* (flesh of the gods). Tim said, "They taught me more about the human psyche in a few hours than all my years as a psychologist." I was, of course, intellectually intrigued.

It was not until the following March that the opportunity presented itself for my first intense psychedelic experience with the psilocybe mushroom. It was profound! It was terrifying! It was blissful! What I hadn't anticipated was that the cost of such aweful wisdom would be involvement. In the course of those few hours, I was catapulted from my safe haven as an intellectual into the middle of the stew of existence.

The journey took me from fascination with the hallucinatory experiences through abject terror as my safe separateness dissolved and finally deposited me in a new and surprising place in my deepest heart where I felt a loving and unbounded merging with all things. I was suddenly "at home" in a world that included all the suffering that I had gone to such lengths to avoid. This seemed like a return to innocence, to the time prior to my being imprisoned in separateness. It was the beginning of my awakening, the start of an intentional spiritual journey.

During the moments I was in these ecstatic states of consciousness, I recognized the innate generosity of my heart and the ease with which one could merge with another's suffering in such a way as to experience it not as her or his suffering but as "our" or "the" suffering. At those moments, even though I felt such an identification with the human condition, there seemed to be no need to protect "myself."

But these experiences of intense unity with the cosmos did not last. As the chemical passed from my nervous system, I was left with only a profound memory. Yet, by treating psychedelics as a sacrament, and using them for spiritual quest, I have learned a great deal over the years.

While many of the psychedelic sessions touched upon compassion, a few now stand out in particular. For example, I was once invited to try a new psychedelic. It was organic, and enthusiasts told me that within nine minutes I would go to the furthest reaches of my mind and return. I am always delighted to experiment, but in each case my decision rests in my trust of the people offering the psychedelic. I felt safe in this living room surrounded by friends.

Within moments of ingesting the chemical, my awareness separated itself from thought and the vastness of pure mind opened before me. I found myself in a familiar place, standing at the edge of the void . . . just one thought away. I recalled the hours as an early adolescent when I would stand at the end of the diving board trying to screw up my courage to try a back dive. One . . . two . . . two and a half . . . two and three-quarters. I hadn't dived then, and I didn't dive into the void now.

A moment more and it was too late. I felt the insistent impetus of the chemical in my brain diminishing. I laughed. It was a joyful laugh, for it acknowledged the awesome pure mind stage upon which who I think I am acts. The laugh also embraced the poignancy of my karmic predicament at the end of the diving board.

Others in the group took their turns ingesting the chemical, one at a time. We were all there for the others. Some cried out joyfully in exaltation of God, others remained silent with secret smiles on their faces. They offered me another opportunity at the end. I accepted.

This time it was different. I saw before me and around me millions upon millions of beings. They were all crying pitifully. My heart was exploding. In my mind's eye I metamorphosed into a huge black woman with great laden breasts. I sat up and reached my arms out to embrace all these suffering beings into myself. They were my children. A cry of agony formed in my bowels. It was not my cry . . . it was the cry of all of our agony. I was retching and dry-heaving with the immensity of the moment. My friends rushed for a bucket, thinking I was about to vomit; there were looks of concern on their faces. But through it all I was in ecstasy. It was the ecstasy of bearing the unbearable, of feeling my breasts give nourishment to all of the children, of merging with a paroxysm of surrender, not this time into the silent void but into the writhing flesh and blood, agonized cry for life itself. It was the ecstasy of being at home in the universe.

And then it was over and I was back. But back now with a memory that takes its place in the gallery of memories that so subtly color the moments that are yet to come.

Another psychedelic memory from years before. I was bearing witness to the multitude . . . they were peasants, perhaps on the Russian steppes. There were untold numbers, and they were all slowly turning a vast wheel. They were chained to the wheel. A feeling of futility and hopelessness pervaded the scene. It seemed to have been going on forever and would so continue. And then I was aware of a golden ring floating just above the heads of these straining beings. Every now and then, out of this vast scene of anguish, I saw an arm raise—a hand, a dirty hand in a torn, fingerless wool glove, reach for the luminous gold ring as it passed. The grasping hand just missed catching hold of the ring. Then the ring passed and the arm was withdrawn in despair.

Why, of the millions of images out of my past, does my internal computer bring this memory up again and again? It has the same quality as the metaphor the Buddha used to describe the rarity and preciousness of a human birth on the wheel of reincarnation. He told of a wooden ox yoke floating in the ocean, and a tortoise swimming in that same vast ocean. The likelihood of the tortoise coming to the surface and finding its head within the yoke is similar to the likelihood of our taking a human birth. The Buddha used this image to goad the monks to appreciate and avail themselves of this precious human birth in order to intensify their efforts for liberation. I always found the metaphor had the opposite effect. It discouraged me and made me want to open a beer and turn on the TV.

Somehow these images, rising out of what Carl Jung would consider our collective unconscious, fit with the vast Hindu expanses of time, measured in *yugas* and *kalpas*—periods of hundreds of thousands of years in which civilizations, even form itself, have come into being and then disappeared. Time spans in which our "recorded history" is but the tiniest, most recent moment. The god Shiva dances, and all the worlds manifest; then he sits in meditation and draws the many shards of mindstuff back into himself. These time frames, and the idea of reincarnation, color my actions. For I see myself and every person as living out our few years on earth as but a moment in our souls' life. It is like the deck of cards that gives the impression of a moving figure as you flip through it with your thumb. Each card, each freeze-frame in the movie—another life. Do these perspectives trivialize life? Not for me. For me they give balance to the inordinately fearful preoccupations we have with *this* life and *this* death.

These experiences meld into a background of consciousness against which I see inequality among lives. There are such obvious differences among people, more than genes and environment, economics and education, can account for. These are karmic differences—differences in agenda because each of us takes birth at a different stage in his or her journey of evolution. A person devoting her or his life to the highest spiritual seeking is no greater or lesser than the being who spends a lifetime in just surviving. One who lives long is no "better" than one who dies young. Each lives out his or her own agenda. The wheel of *dharma* (the law) turns. Of course, understanding all this is not grounds for justifying injustice, but these insights are part of the body of wisdom that must be embraced if we are to alleviate the scourge of injustice with skillful means.

In the years from 1961 to 1967, through many hundreds of ingestions of a great variety of mind-altering substances, I entered again and again into that blissful unitive feeling, often having to pass once again through the stages of terror as I lost the safety of distance, but I was never able to integrate this feeling of identity with all things into the rest of my life. As many times as I tasted the nectar, that many times I was cast back into my separateness and the lonely isolation behind the walls of intellect. Hearing of this persistence, and my willingness to undergo such often frightening experiences voluntarily, you can possibly appreciate the intensity of my yearning to escape what G. I. Gurdjieff, the Russian philosopher-mystic, called "the prison of our mind."

I was suffering intensely because of my feeling of entrapment in my own separateness. If I had never ingested psychedelics and tasted the unity of all things, I might not have suffered so badly. But once I saw the possibility of escape, I was driven onward.

It was this yearning most of all, and the awakening realization that, while psychedelics might show the possibility, they weren't going to free me, that drove me in 1967 to journey to the East. I had read so many books from the East that seemed to provide maps for escape, but I felt the need to find a living cartographer.

In India, it was only after six months, when I had given up the search, that I met my guru, Neem Karoli Baba. (I refer to him as Maharajji, a common name of honor given to an elder or spiritual being in India.) Within an hour of our first meeting, he had taken me beyond my mind, and opened my heart. It was clear that I had found the guide I was looking for. I remained with him for the winter in the foothills of the Himalayas. My staying was never discussed in so many words. He just arranged for me to be housed in a small temple compound in a valley nearby and to receive food and instruction in *raja yoga*.

I almost always find myself somewhat shy in speaking to Westerners about the relationship between my guru and myself. First of all, Westerners have a very difficult time with the idea of surrendering to another person, as a *chela* or disciple does to a guru. It is often seen as a sign of weakness or neurotic behavior. In fact, I myself had viewed it that way in the past. Aren't gurus, after all, just good (and sometimes bad) mother or father surrogates into whom we project divinity?

When I first met Maharajji, I would not bow to touch his feet. The gesture smacked of surrender, rather like giving one's power away. Later I found out that touching a guru's feet has very little to do with surrender. It is merely acknowledging that the other being is a high being. And it is thought that a guru exudes spiritual vibrations that make even the dust from his or her feet like sacred ash, i.e., ashes left from a sacred fire. So, for one's own benefit, one takes the dust, symbolically, by touching the feet and then placing the dust on one's own head as *prasad,* or spiritual food.

I found in Maharajji such seamless wisdom and compassion, such clarity of perception born of true freedom, and the absence of any need on his part to exploit me, that surrender came naturally and easily. I did not experience that I was surrendering to another ego. He was free, even of being "somebody." It wasn't as if I was surrendering to Maharajji, the man. Rather I was surrendering to the truth and love that came through him. It was a surrender that took no effort because it was in harmony with a truth that I already acknowledged in my soul. Such surrender is spoken of in the spiritual literature as "the surrender that is no surrender." A great Indian spiritual master, Ramana Maharshi, once said, "God, Guru, and Self are ultimately One." If that is the case, then when one is surrendering, whether to God, Guru, or deepest Self, one is actually surrendering into the One that lies within and beyond the Many.

When I think of Maharajji, I immediately experience a wave of love, as though I am being immersed in an ocean of love. His presence at that moment is not just a reminder of love, it *is* the love that seems to sweep away the cobwebs of inadequacy, impotency, doubt, and fear left by the spider demon host, who hover, waiting for the moment of forgetfulness, when once again you forget that you are in love.

After Maharajji left his body in 1973, there was no longer an external source to turn to in order to receive his guidance and tune to his wisdom. I had to dive within myself and begin to trust my own intuition heard in times of meditative quiet. There have been very few instances during this time when I have had actual visions of him. Generally it is more subtle. I just go into the deepest place in my heart and stay there. At those moments I feel as if he has not forgotten me. That sounds funny, even to write, but it's true. He once said to me, "I am always in communion with you." At another time he said, "Whoever thinks of me, I am with them."

In that way, he comes to mind hundreds of times each day, showing some facet, some quality or other, perhaps discriminative wisdom or patience, compassion or emptiness, joy or childlikeness, ancient elderness or jokester-tricksterness. Each time he is a reminder. But of what? Usually of the fact that things aren't the way I thought they were. So each time I think of him and my heart opens, I experience him being there in my life situation with and for me, like an imaginary playmate, and we enjoy together the outrageous *lila* (game) to which I find myself privy. Often I am not quiet enough to hear him, but that doesn't stop me from listening as best as I can, again and again, to hear "his slightest whisper above earth's loudest song."

When I think about Maharajji, what frequently comes to mind is a story about him. As an act of love, I, along with other devotees, collected thousands of these stories and read and reread and thought about them many times. In 1978 we published a thousand of them in a book, *Miracle of Love.* The stories goad me to examine the "stuff" of my mind.

For example, in the book we recounted the story of Maharajji walking with an old devotee. At one point Maharajji looks up into the sky and says that So-and-so, an old lady devotee, has just died; then he laughs. His devotee is shocked by this news and says, "Are you some kind of a butcher, laughing at someone's death?" Maharajji looks surprised and retorts, "Would you rather have me make believe I'm one of the puppets?" Such a story, which I've worked with over the years, knowing that Maharajji did not say things idly, suggests that we, who are unwittingly acting out a script like puppets, approach the drama of death as very real. I find that this story strengthens my faith that all is not as it seems—even suffering and death. There are other planes of reality in which the deeper karmic significance is evident. To live simultaneously in those planes as well as in the one in which suffering and death are all too real changes the meaning and thus our reactions to everything.

Here's another story that pushes the same buttons in me. When the chaos was occurring in Bangladesh in the early seventies, I wanted to take my VW bus there because I had a romantic image of serving as an ambulance driver. I was very upset about the immense suffering. But Maharajji was calm. Finally he said to me, "Don't you see that it's all perfect?" I owned that I didn't see that at all. He looked sad and patient. Obviously he could see what I could not. Maharajji didn't say that I shouldn't feel pain at the suffering, or that I shouldn't go to help. He was simply reminding me not to lose sight of other planes of reality where the perspective was indeed different.

This same message is in the *Bhagavad Gita,* where Arjuna is overwhelmed by the impending war in which he is going to be called upon to kill his cousins, preceptors, and friends whom circumstance has placed on the opposing side. He throws down his bow and refuses to fight. Lord Krishna, who is serving as Arjuna's charioteer, says he must do his duty—play his part. Then Krishna opens Arjuna's third eye and shows him other planes of reality. Arjuna sees Krishna as a vast being into whose open mouth armies are rushing headlong, pouring like a river of humanity back into him. Arjuna is so distressed by what he sees that he begs Krishna to return his normal vision.

That story is often seen as an endorsement of war. Whether it is taken that way—or seen metaphorically, as by Vivekananda and Gandhi, for the inner battle—the experience of Arjuna reminds us that, as we try to discover what our path in life might be, we must keep in mind that there is more to reality than the obvious. The deeper my appreciation of this truth, the less reactive, though not necessarily less responsive, I find myself in the presence of the suffering of others.

Back in 1967–68, I was practicing many hours of hatha yoga, doing intense breathing exercises, meditating, fasting, chanting the names of God, and studying spiritual texts. In the course of those practices and studies, I came to understand that the spiritual journey requires freeing oneself from identification with all desires. I couldn't see how it would be possible to do this in the marketplace of life, where the power of these desires, both gross and subtle, cannot be confronted directly. I decided that the only way to extricate the mind from identification was to withdraw to a place where the opportunity to satisfy these desires would be absent.

Swami Vivekananda, who interprets the *Bhagavad Gita* as an allegory for the internal struggle that is part and parcel of liberation, describes it thus:

> Arrayed against him, Arjuna, the seeker, finds the army of his desires. Not just the desires that are conventionally considered evil but many others too: the desire for harmless enjoyment, the desire to shine in society surrounded by friends, and the desire to lead a secure and comfortable life. These and many more have taken the field against the soul . . . under the leadership of various ideals. The call of the blood, the prestige of habit and established custom, the glittering ideals of family affection, patriotism, and of devotion to religion . . . must be relinquished even though they have served as guides and teachers in the past.

This stage of my spiritual life was happening during the years of the civil rights and anti–Vietnam War actions. After the early sixties, during which hundreds of thousands of us had opened to new perceptions of reality and new possibilities, the directions of our lives seemed to diverge. Some of us saw the obvious limits of the social institutions of our society, and the ways in which they perpetuate injustice. With this new sense of psychedelically awakened individual empowerment, these people set about changing the society, with what was basically a revolutionary state of mind.

Others, of which I was one, saw that the root of suffering lies deep in the individual psyche, and that inner work must precede attempts to change the outer world. Until we change ourselves, any actions we perform will simply create more karma. Reaction will follow action in never-ending cycles, resulting, in the long term, in the perpetuation of suffering.

Still others saw that one must do inner and outer work at the same time. I recall when I was in India receiving a letter from Allen Ginsberg full of clippings about violence at demonstrations in Chicago. It was clear that Allen, who was chanting "Om" in the middle of riots, was attempting to combine his inner and outer work. I marveled at his courage, knowing that I was not made of such stuff. At another time Alan Watts took me aside and suggested that I was too attached to emptiness and should come back into the world.

Despite the seductions of the opportunity to participate in the shaping of world events, I chose to stay quiet and follow a very strict renunciate path. When I returned to India in late 1970, that was my path, and meditation was the center of it. I had made arrangements with a fine meditation master to study with him during the monsoons the following summer in Kosani, a mountain village perhaps sixty miles east of the temple where I often stayed with Maharajji.

When I was able to meet Maharajji in early '71, I told him that I was planning to continue my meditation study the following summer. I expected him to praise me for my commitment to practice, but all he said was "If you desire." That disquieted me. He seemed to be treating my serious spiritual intent as a mere whim. I decided to ignore his remark and go ahead with my summer plans.

During the next six months, Maharajji said nothing more about the plan. When summer came along and I announced that four of us were going to study meditation, he seemed pleased. But, as it turned out, after we were settled in Kosani, the meditation teacher sent a telegram saying that because of family illness he would not be coming to join us. At the same time, some thirty Westerners mysteriously arrived in Kosani, having been sent by Maharajji to "be with Ram Dass." I could hear him laughing at me. So I surrendered and spent the summer running an ashram of devotion, study, yoga, and some meditation. Instead of meditating, I had ended up doing service.

When we returned to Maharajji, he giggled, called me "meditation teacher," and seemed delighted with the whole turn of events. I was frustrated by the absence of the meditation master, and I questioned Maharajji about the value of meditation. He said, "Meditation is good. If you bring your mind to one point, you will know God." But he still never let me meditate when I was around him.

In those years, I did indeed quiet my mind somewhat. As a result, I developed some perceptual clarity. However, what I saw with this new clarity was that I was caught in what I have come to call the "horny celibate syndrome." I was deeply attached to *not* having desires. I was still afraid.

Allen Ginsberg once called me and asked me to sit in for him at an antinuclear rally at Rocky Flats, Colorado. He had to be in New York and had heard I was scheduled to be lecturing in Boulder, Colorado, the day after the demonstration. I had been waiting for the situation when it would feel right to let myself into the river of political activism and dissent. This felt just right. A group of young Western Buddhists would be sitting in meditation in the middle of the rally, and I was invited to bring a *zafu* (pillow) and join them.

A light, misty rain was falling, and the gathering of several thousand people out by the factory that made the trigger mechanisms that activated the nuclear bombs reminded me of a sixties be-in in San Francisco's Golden Gate Park. We meditators, perhaps twenty of us, sat in a circle. I crossed my legs, pulled my jacket around me, and settled in for a long "sit." Snatches of conversation caught my attention as people passed by close around us. Then the speeches started from the stage. I was sinking into deeper meditation, yet everything around me was clear . . . luminously clear.

A leading antinuclear activist was speaking. I felt the caring in her heart as she spoke of her children and the desire that they grow up in a world free from deadly radiation. In her voice was melded the cry of the mother, the anger of the outraged feminist who was furious with the men who had gotten us into this predicament, the urgency of the pediatrician-scientist who saw probabilities with an apprehensive eye. Her message was clear: "Fear! Urgency! Act!" I could feel her charisma and the immediacy and relevance of her message drawing the crowd into agreement.

Hearing her words from my meditation cushion, I sensed her mind pulling me into a definition of reality that seemed constricted, tight. I felt that she was engaging the audience through their insecurities. Noble as her intent might have been, she was manipulating her audience as "them." What she was doing appeared old-fashioned to me. I knew that it is possible to engage an audience as "us"—quietly seeing together how things are, leaving to each person the responsibility for subsequent individual actions.

I became sad. Maybe getting people politically activated requires fanning the flames of fear and urgency, of moral outrage and the need to *do something*. Perhaps you and I just opening to how it is in the universe, then doing whatever we see fit about it, trusting one another to act in accordance with our deepest truth, is not enough. But I don't believe that. If we must give up our respect for one another's inner wisdom and coerce and manipulate one another for the greater good, then it seems a rather hollow victory to me.

There was another thing that made me sad as I listened to the speeches. I felt sad that we were still polarizing the world into the good guys and the bad guys, then getting our adrenaline rush from feelings of righteous indignation. Weren't we ready to acknowledge that reality is a conspiracy in which we all play our part? Didn't the planes and cars that we used to get to this rally use the very fossil fuel that feeds the fear- and greed-driven economic political policies that dominate the mind connected to the hand that could push the button that would create the nuclear conflagration?

In the many times since Rocky Flats that I have spoken at peace rallies or participated in demonstrations, I have remembered Mohandas Gandhi and Martin Luther King, Jr., who opposed injustice, irrationality, and lack of caring with firmness and confrontation. Yet they did so with open hearts, with a compassion that embraced all us poor, misguided mortals, friend and foe alike. Gandhi said, "The British must be forced to leave India, but I want them to leave as friends." And King said, "Love is the only force capable of transforming an enemy into a friend."

Be Like Gandhi

In retrospect, it's interesting to see that, from the very beginning of my relationship with Maharajji, he was guiding me toward the spiritual path of service. It is now clear why I wasn't able to hear him. Service lacks glamour as a path. It lacks romance. I wanted esoteric teachings, secret mantras, mystical initiations, meditations in Himalayan caves. I was really fascinated by what Trungpa Rinpoche called "spiritual materialism."

Also, the difficulty I was facing in accepting service as a path to liberation revolved around my attitude toward life itself. It really wasn't until the midseventies, over fifteen years after I had consciously begun my spiritual journey, that I acknowledged how deeply caught I had become in my aversion to human incarnation, to the psychophysical world of existence. As a result of my various practices, I was able to move in and out of planes of reality in which I experienced rapture, bliss, and equanimity. I had become addicted to these planes and was remaining aloof from life.

Taking a human birth still seemed like an error—a monstrous error! I was obviously too pure to belong among all these rascals and brigands who were caught in greed and hatred, sloth, agitation, and doubt. The "earth plane" appeared to be little more than an ocean of suffering, best avoided. So to choose a path that led me into or through the world seemed very unappealing.

Seeing the strength of this aversion, I was finally awakened to the distinction between getting "high" and becoming "free." I knew how to get high, which involves overriding or pushing away the world. But under those conditions I wasn't free. And I saw that what I really wanted was freedom, not just another high. Highs are part of the world of polarities. What goes up comes down. The deeper requirement would be to be at peace and happy whether high or low, whether in the world or out of it.

To fulfill this requirement, I would have to face my aversion to incarnation squarely. After all, my incarnation was my karma made manifest. As such, my life was my curriculum. It presented me at every moment with one or another of my attractions or aversions. Only when I could deal with the unfolding of my unique karma without getting lost in identification with my attractions or aversions would I be free. While setting aside worldly concerns had helped me become rooted in another plane, thus giving me some measure of spiritual perspective, I couldn't stay there indefinitely. As the yogis say, "There is *no* place to stand."

In addition, I had to admit that the path of renunci-
ation and austerity wasn't really working. Through it, I
was getting new clarity and depth, but I wasn't becoming free—just more uptight. Acknowledging all of these
fascinations, aversions, and frustrations finally opened my
mind enough to hear how Maharajji had been guiding
me. I recalled that the day after I met him, we were
together again. He was sitting on a stone wall. When I
came before him, he looked at me quizzically and asked,
"You know Gandhi?"

"I didn't know him personally, but I know of him," I
said. And I added, "He was a great saint." (I used the
word *saint,* which has a far less specialized meaning in
India than in the West. In India, it means "a very good
or saintly person.")

"Yes!" Maharajji said. "You be like Gandhi."

"I'd like to be," I said. Then he hit me on the head and
laughed. The hit was less than a clout but definitely more
than a tap. Perhaps he was realigning my neural path-
ways. Perhaps setting a thought form in motion, perhaps
who knows what!

Over the years I read a great deal about Mahatma
Gandhi. I found Gandhi to be an extraordinary blend of
the appreciation of the inner life and superlative social
action. He was able to integrate inner spiritual work,
sensitivity to the suffering of the poor and disenfranchised, and masterful use of skillful political means to
bring about social change.

The most brilliant example, to my mind, of the coming together of all the strands of compassion in Gandhi
was the salt march. You may recall that the British had

become increasingly repressive and greedy regarding their India colony. They had even imposed an intolerable tax on salt and required people to purchase salt at highly inflated prices through government channels, even though salt was readily available cheaply through Indian salt mines. The Indians, being hardworking dwellers in the semitropics, needed salt. About 20 percent of the income of poor Indians would be required—just for salt.

Officials from the Congress party, of which Gandhi was the moral force and political strategist, came to him and requested a plan of opposition to the British. Gandhi said he'd have to meditate upon the matter. Again and again, week after week, the party leaders returned to Gandhi's ashram, but it was only after several months, when the officials had become thoroughly irritated with what looked like Gandhi's stalling techniques, that a plan became clear to him. He explained his simple strategy to them. Then he picked up his staff and started walking toward the sea. He walked for twenty-four days and two hundred miles, and along the way thousands joined him. On the evening of the day they finally arrived at the edge of the ocean, he led the group in prayer. In the morning he bathed in the water. Then, coming up the beach to an area where there was a natural salt deposit from the ocean, he reached down and picked up a handful of salt. By this simple act he defied the British Empire, for, in effect, he was mining his own salt. Within a month, 100,000 people had followed his example and were in jail for breaking the law. And the momentum grew and grew. Gandhi had found such a simple form of peaceful civil disobedience, a form that the most uneducated Indian could understand, through which he was able to unleash a vast human moral power to throw off the oppressor.

I didn't see much similarity between Gandhi and myself. I acquired steel-rimmed spectacles like those Gandhi wore, but I saw that I really couldn't imitate him. I wasn't about to spin my own cloth or live on a diet of goat's milk and almonds, or travel around dressed in a loincloth. I was a Westerner living with an entirely different set of experiences and opportunities. It would take me some time to understand at a deeper level what Maharajji had meant by the injunction "Be like Gandhi." All I recognized was that it had something to do with participating in the human condition.

Also during my first visit to India, in 1967, I was told that Maharajji had given me the name Ram Dass. I had no idea what it meant since I understood neither Hindi nor Hindu mythology. So I asked naïvely, "Is that good?" And I was assured that it was very good. It was translated to me as "Servant of God."

It turned out that Ram Dass is another name for the Hindu monkey god, Hanuman, about whom I also knew nothing. Before meeting Maharajji, I had not been at all attracted to Hinduism. Quite the contrary! It seemed rather gauche, with its bad calendar art, fluorescently lit temples, and huge throngs of devotees pushing and screaming. The rather austere quiet of the Buddhism I encountered in India seemed far more sane and appealing.

When I met my guru, it was certainly not the Hindu setting in which I met him that was so appealing to me. It was his presence, his love, his compassion, and his wisdom that touched me in a way that no human being had ever touched me before. Yet I did meet him at a Hindu temple in which the central deity was the monkey god Hanuman. It seemed paradoxical that a being in whom I felt such infinite wisdom was in some way connected to a monkey god. Indeed, it rather embarrassed me. Finally I dealt with it in my mind by concluding that my guru was way beyond monkey gods and such but supported such idolatry for the benefit of the simple folk who lived in the region.

During that first winter, I was alone a great deal. When I was not doing my practices or study and was bored, I found myself sitting before the statue of Hanuman. The humor of my predicament did not escape me. After attaining a Ph.D. at Stanford and serving as a professor at Harvard, here I was sitting at the feet of a painted marble monkey. I was sure that if my old colleagues could see me, beaded and bearded, worshiping a monkey, they would undoubtedly conclude that the psychedelic chemicals I had experimented with had pushed me over the edge. And I wasn't at all certain that they wouldn't be right. But it didn't matter. I felt that I was finding in the Hindu lineage the purifications and practices that I needed in order to integrate the various planes of consciousness that had up to this time remained so separate from one another.

Part of these practices involved reading more deeply in Hindu literature. In the course of these readings, I came across a list of nine aspects of devotion to God. For example, one could relate to God as mother to child, as in the case of Mary to Jesus. Or the relationship could be as child to father, as Jehovah is often portrayed. Or as lover and beloved, as in the case of Krishna and Radha. And there in the list was that relationship to God of servant to master, as exemplified by Hanuman and Ram. I was reminded of Paul's injunction in the New Testament to "be confirmed in love through service." Well and good that I was named after Hanuman; at that time I still could not see service as in any way connected to my liberation.

During that first winter in India, when I was wrestling with all this confusion, a wonderful new Indian friend, K. K. Sah, brought me an English-translation copy of the *Ramayana,* a book that he promised would help me understand Hanuman. It was a folk version written by the poet Tulsidas. The great epic poem the *Ramayana* is a bible for millions of people in India. The people hear it recited, study it, name their children after its characters, and model their lives on the teachings contained in its stories. In fact, in 1989, when the *Ramayana* was broadcast on television for a half hour each Sunday morning throughout India, everyone just stopped to watch it. Even the trains and buses stopped as the drivers refused to drive until they had seen the latest installment. It was a difficult book for me initially because it is so lushly devotional, with page after page of adulation for one character or another. Tulsidas was clearly an ecstatic and was writing for the eyes and hearts of believers. But I plugged away at it and finally began to find out just who this monkey was.

Basically, the story, like most bibles, is about the battle between good and evil. Ram is an incarnation of God who compassionately takes birth in order to rid the universe of the *rakshashas* (demons) led by Ravana, the very egotistical demon king who has ten heads and twenty arms. At one point Ram, his wife, Sita, and his devoted brother Lakshman are living in the jungle as hermits. Ravana, true to his demon nature of lust and greed, steals Sita away by cleverly diverting Ram's and Lakshman's attention with a wild deer chase. Ravana magically flies with Sita through the air to his stronghold in Sri Lanka, where he imprisons her and threatens her with death unless she accepts his advances.

Ram and Lakshman then set out to find Sita. In this they are aided by the monkey and bear tribes. Among the monkeys, Hanuman is the most pure in his devotion to Ram and Ram's cause. As a result of his single-minded devotion, Hanuman is blessed with extraordinary powers, which he uses in carrying out the mission Ram has assigned him. It is Hanuman who, after leaping across the ocean, finally finds Sita. And, throughout the remainder of the story, Hanuman again and again performs extraordinary feats in helping Ram to be victorious in his battle against evil and in his efforts to bring Sita back and to uphold *Dharma* (the Truth). Hanuman is characterized as a wise and rascally monkey whose joy is found in serving Ram. He is so close to Ram, serving him so intimately, that he is known as the "breath of Ram."

For several years after being named after Hanuman, I kept pictures of my guru and Hanuman around. I was getting to like the idea of being a servant of God, although I still had no idea what it meant for me.

In 1971, during my second trip to India, Maharajji once again cryptically gave me the message about service. At one point I asked him how I could become enlightened. Maharajji said, "Serve everyone." The answer was hardly the one that I had expected, so I assumed something had gotten lost in translation. At the next opportunity I tried a different tack and asked him how I could know God. He replied, "Feed everyone." In my snobbish, elitist view, service was a lesser vehicle than meditation and the more esoteric spiritual practices of which I'd read. Instead of the kind of practices the "big people" did, I was being encouraged only to feed and serve people.

Maharajji also encouraged me to study the *Bhagavad Gita*. In 1974 I went to the Arizona desert to meditate and study the *Gita* in preparation for teaching a course at the opening of the Naropa Institute in Boulder, Colorado. I pored through nine translations of the *Gita* and came to appreciate its incredible profundity as a spiritual treatise. While the *Gita* gives important instruction about the inner practices for the transformation of the mind and the heart, its major thrust is the path of selfless service *(nish kam karma yoga)*.

In the dialogue in the *Gita*, Krishna (the voice of absolute wisdom) instructs Arjuna (the seeker) to do his duty in the world but dedicate the fruits of his actions to God. Arjuna is enjoined to become an instrument of Dharma. As such he would not lay claim to either his actions or their outcome. Indeed, he would perform his duty as impeccably as possible as an offering to the higher spirit. Through such one-pointedness in his acts in the world, he would come to God or union. Thus the name *karma yoga*, coming to union through living out one's karma. Another way of saying this would be that one makes one's *karma* (the situation in which one finds oneself as a result of past actions) into one's *dharma* (the word *dharma* means the path to liberation, as well as the liberating truth itself). To be liberated is not to leave the world, but to remain in the world and not be identified with it.

This instruction to consecrate all one's acts as a way of approaching God is the message of many spiritual teachers and religious traditions. For example, in Mahayana Buddhism, it is said: "The way is not one of running away from the world, but of overcoming it through growing knowledge (*prajna*), through active love (*maitri*) toward one's fellow beings, through inner participation in the joys and sufferings of others (*karuna, mudita*) and equanimity with regard to one's own weal and woe (*upekha*)."

Eventually all Maharajji's messages started to get through to me: "Be like Gandhi. . . . Your name is Ram Dass [Hanuman]. . . . Do your duty in the world as a way of serving God. . . . Feed everyone. . . . Serve everyone." Maharajji was telling me, whether I liked it or not, that my path was karma yoga, and that the specific actions were to be those of service.

I have described these stages of my own spiritual journey in some detail because as I look at what has influenced my attempts to relieve suffering in others, I see that the journey toward freedom remains a key impetus. That may sound harsh or self-centered, but perhaps if I say that my yearning for freedom is altruistically based, that it is motivated by the bodhisattva's seeking of enlightenment for the benefit of all beings, it sounds better. And it is true that the spiritual motivation has in it the objective of relieving suffering for all beings, since we are all interconnected, or even a unity. Still, there is a selfish component to *sadhana* (spiritual practice). Even Gandhi, who espoused selfless service, when acclaimed for his actions in helping a village said, "I didn't do it for them. I did it for *my own sadhana.*"

Selfless service cannot come out of a denial of a personal motivation and objective. Even though you really care about others and want to help them, your spiritual journey is your own, determined by your unique karma. It is only at the conclusion of the journey that, as Ramakrishna says, you throw into the fire both the thorn (attachments) removed from your foot and the thorn (spiritual practice) you used to remove the other thorn. Only then, when, as Gandhi says, the surrender to God is complete, does true selfless service emerge. Because, of course, at that point you have seen through the mind-generated nature of the idea of "self" itself, and even the personal desire for enlightenment has fallen away.

When I acknowledged that karma yoga was my path, I looked about to see which service to perform. Wouldn't appropriate service in some way be connected with the facts of my incarnation: that I was born in this particular body, to this family, in this socioeconomic class, in this country, in this ecosystem, at this time in history? What was my work with the other incarnates? How was I involved with their suffering?

As I re-viewed my life since meeting Maharajji, I realized that in fact I was already serving in this way. I was writing books and giving lectures, and these were apparently helping others.

Thousands of people have told me how one of my books (usually it's *Be Here Now*) has changed their lives. The ones I meet all seem to be relatively happy about the way it's changed their lives, even though I meet them in surprisingly disparate roles in society. One is now a Jesuit priest, one I met in the prison in Denpasar, Bali, and another is a guard. There is an industrialist, a mother of five, a judge, and a dealer of grass. There is a rock singer, an actor, a student, and a street hustler. A Hindu boy in India told me his grandfather reads *Be Here Now.* There's an old Hawaiian and a young Tibetan monk, spiritual teachers, rabbis, a mortician, doctors, and some of the homeless. The list goes on and on. Recently I met a Western woman who had become a Buddhist nun. She was quiet, had humor in her eyes, and was vibrant with life force. She bowed and said, "I just want to thank you. When I was at my lowest in the States I read one of your books and it turned my life around. And all these years I've been deepening my practice and sending you blessings for having helped me."

I know that it sounds disgustingly ego-y to be describing adulation of myself and reciting such a list, but it doesn't feel that way inside. Because I don't feel that I really wrote any of those books, thus I do not experience these people as speaking to me, personally. The way the books came to be was that at one point Hari Das, who was the yogi Maharajji had instructed to teach me yoga, wrote on his slate (he was *maun,* or silent), "Maharajji has just given his *ashirbad* for your book." "What is *ashirbad*?" I wanted to know, "and what book?"

Hari Das explained that *ashirbad* means "blessing," and that it was for whatever book I wrote. So when *Be Here Now,* after a journey of publisher rejections, finally came into being and touched millions of people, all I personally felt was gracefully used by Maharajji to reassure so many hearts that the intuitive truths we know are indeed real, even if all the world acts as if they aren't. He was giving them a booster shot of faith with his book, which he had let me write.

But he has never fully convinced me that I am really an author. They are *his* books, from which I, along with the readers, reap the fruits. The fruits for each person are obviously different. The books confront *me* with people's appreciation, with fame and respect; they provide some economic support for me and for causes in which I believe, as well as helping me to understand more deeply what I know by writing about it. All of these things are blessings if you are not attached to or needful of them. But if you are attached to any of them, then the fruits of authorship become a hot flame of purification. And that fire is another kind of grace. I've been burned a number of times by that fire too.

The number of opportunities to relieve suffering is as great as the number of sufferings themselves. How then can I decide which sufferings get my attention and which don't? Which letters get a phone call? Which needy non-profit organizations do I perform benefits for? Which teachings should I take? How, indeed, do I live a life of service? Such decisions cannot be based solely on rational considerations. I recognize that my actions are based on intuition and the existential situation in which I find myself, which for each of us is unique.

So, in the seventies, as I looked at what specific actions my karma yoga would embrace, I saw that what I had to offer others was what I had gleaned from my spiritual training. I felt others had preempted the world of helping with regard to physical suffering: others were better cooks, had been trained as nurses or medical technicians, were skilled in designing wells, chemical toilets, solar heating, or forest usage, were shrewd in traversing the byways of bureaucracy and politics, could fight injustice in the courts, express their compassion with epidemiological curves and computers, or plan and execute an act of civil disobedience better than I.

What I could do was keep focusing on the ignorance that lies at the very root of suffering. Again and again, in one way or another, I could enunciate the Buddha's Four Noble Truths about suffering and its end. That is, I could serve as a spiritual friend or teacher and share practices that could help others see their own suffering for what it was, dependent upon their own mind states. Once seeing this linkage, they could begin to change their mind states in a way that would free them from suffering.

Of course, the only people who would even acknowledge the relevance of such help would be people who wanted to awaken. As Gurdjieff pointed out, "We are caught in the prison of the mind. If we are to escape we must recognize that we are in prison. If we think we are free, then no escape is possible." So the population that I would serve was defined by their conscious intention to become free.

During those years I think I felt that without the leverage created by the desire to awaken in another person, helping that person to escape one suffering just seemed to make space for the next suffering to appear. It seemed endless or, at least, went on until the person started to awaken. Once this began to happen, a person learned to use his or her suffering as grist for the mill for further awakening, thus, ultimately, becoming free from suffering itself. But, until then, there seemed to be a certain futility in helping an unawakened person.

Now, as I look back at those attitudes, I see how rooted in fear they were. I was afraid of the massive unawakened suffering of the world. I was afraid that if I opened myself to it, I would drown. To protect myself, I needed the boundary definition that "I work only with people who want to awaken." I felt pity for others, and I was willing to help from a distance with a donation of money or even time, but, basically, I had no direct business with the suffering mass of humanity.

The fear I was experiencing was strikingly exemplified in the second or third meeting of a class on compassionate action that had been convened at the Cathedral of St. John the Divine in New York City. The class was jointly sponsored by the cathedral, the Seva Foundation, the Open Center, and radio station WBAI. There were, perhaps, two hundred of us who had come together to engage the issue of homelessness. We had all agreed that during the course we would each in one way or another help alleviate the plight of homeless folks in the city. Some of us volunteered to cook and serve in soup kitchens; some to monitor overnight shelters in church basements; some to lobby against unfair housing practices such as warehousing empty apartments, or legislation that unfairly benefited the real estate developers; some to work on the streets with mental patients who had gotten lost between the bureaucratic cracks; some to help the men and women living on the streets to unify, organize, and stage demonstrations to bring attention to their plight. We were to keep diaries of our experiences and share the entries at an open microphone at each class, so that we could increase our collective awareness of the ways in which we were both the problem and the solution in the ever-worsening homelessness situation.

One woman explained that she had chosen to work in a shelter or a soup kitchen (I don't recall which), but that her diary entry did not involve that activity. Rather she wanted to share an experience she had had right outside her apartment building. She explained that during the past many months, as she left her apartment to go either to the bus or to the store, she would pass the same man begging at the corner of her street. He had a paper coffee cup with a few coins in it, which he would jiggle as each person went by. The woman reported that sometimes she would put a quarter in the cup and sometimes she wouldn't. After telling us this, she smiled in some embarrassment and admitted that she had evolved a sort of budget for her giving to him—$2.50 per week. She said that she regularly spread the giving of the money out over the week.

"As a result of this course," she said, "I realized that, though I gave him money, I had never *really* acknowledged his existence as a fellow human being. When I examined why that was, I saw that I was afraid. But what was I afraid of? I wasn't afraid that he was going to rape me or anything like that. I wasn't even afraid he might take my purse. After all, we had been passing each other regularly all this time. "No," she said, "what I was afraid of was that, if I opened up to him, he'd end up living in my apartment."

In the discussion that followed the reflective and empathetic silence her remark elicited in the group, we saw the abstract issue involved. We were afraid of our own hearts' caring. We were afraid that, if we truly opened our hearts to the suffering of the people around us, we would be unable to set limits.

During the seventies, when I defined my service as only relevant for those wishing to awaken, I, along with some friends, started the Hanuman Foundation, an organization that would serve as an umbrella for various spiritual service projects. The two major projects begun at that time were the Prison-Ashram Project and the Dying Project.

Why those two projects? Partly, because those two populations were available to me. After I had been thrown out of Harvard for psychedelic research, society was hardly about to trust me with its children or any of the movers and shakers in the power structure. I guess people figured I couldn't do a great deal of damage to the prison population or the dying.

We had received so many letters from inmates in various federal and state prisons who wanted to use their "time" in a way that would help their spiritual development. The Prison-Ashram Project was designed to offer that population spiritual support and guidance through books, lectures, workshops, pen pal clubs, and so on. The project, under the leadership of Bo and Sita Lozoff, served many, many inmates through these vehicles.

As a result of my study of Tibetan Buddhism, particularly the *Bardo Thödol,* or Tibetan Book of the Dead, I had recognized that the state of one's consciousness at the moment of the death of the body is spiritually crucial. Our society not only doesn't focus on that moment but goes out of its way to deny the whole matter of death.

The Dying Project was an attempt to address this issue by focusing on death and dying from a spiritual point of view. Stephen Levine, later joined by his wife, Ondrea, carried this project to incredible heights of compassionate service through books, tapes, workshops, and telephone and personal visits. And Dale Borglum, at one point, created the Dying Center in New Mexico.

Both of these projects, you can see, were initially focused exclusively for people—inmates on the one hand and people with terminal illnesses on the other—who wished to use their karmic predicament as a spiritual practice to help them awaken. These projects were, in their early days, not relevant to either the general prison population or the general dying population. Later, when I was no longer directly connected with the projects, they broadened their mandates considerably.

Reflecting on that period and the times from the early sixties up to then, I see that I and many of my associates were often impatient with other people's suffering. We had found in Eastern literature excellent maps of human consciousness, maps that spelled out the cause of suffering. We felt that we had "seen through" suffering, and we were impatient with those who hadn't.

This attitude made me very selective about those to whom I made myself available. For example, I had learned over the years the folly of visiting Person A at the behest of Person B. Unless Person A truly wanted to visit with me, I had no real license to ask that we work together to awaken out of suffering. Without that license, our time together would often degenerate into a rather superficial hanging out that, while perhaps "nice," felt minimally useful. In some instances I would attempt to use power to force awakening. But you can't really do that to other people. You might make them "high" for a moment or two, but unless they are "ready," whatever that might mean, it won't last. So over the years, having had many such experiences, I became very tough about whom I would work with and whom I would not.

When I think about it, however, I realize that I have been approached so many times by people who said that they were interested in spiritual growth. They said all the right things, but, when we got down to it, they really didn't want to let go of their personality dramas. I slowly learned that you have to listen to more than the words in assessing what another person is really asking.

While I kept my distance from most people's life dramas, when I found people who truly yearned to awaken, I was only too delighted to put up with whatever personality or physical "stuff" they might have. Often I would find myself reactive to them, and we would together work happily with my "stuff" as well.

I have a friend, Kelly Niles, who is a quadriplegic. He cannot speak—he only makes sounds—but with help he can communicate through an electronic alphabet board. Kelly is thirty-one and has been like this since an accident when he was eleven.

Initially it was very difficult for me to be with Kelly without reacting to his predicament. He was often caught in anger and self-pity, and in his presence I found myself masking my own pity, sadness, guilt, and anger about his body. So my visits with him all had a slight edge of hysteria. But over time, as I got to know Kell better and better, and shared my reactions openly, our relationship changed. I noticed his infirmity less and less. I began to be with the consciousness behind his melodrama; a beautiful, delightful, and wise being was there—someone with whom I could look at all the sufferings; his and mine, Kell with his crippled body and frustrated sex life; me with my uptight mind and all my "problems." And, as a result of this work together, Kell felt heard by me, and I felt heard by him. Now we have moments of great peace and joy together. The relationship has been healing to both of us.

Just how extraordinary Kell's inner being is was demonstrated when I invited him to introduce me at a lecture I was giving in Santa Rosa to healers of one stripe or another. The audience was noisily greeting one another, but when Kell was wheeled onto the stage, his body contorted, saliva coming from his mouth, everything stopped. The audience didn't know what was happening. Then Kell started with his alphabet board and said simply, "R.D. says we are not our bodies. Amen!" It was the best one-liner I could imagine—complete as it was with humor, wisdom, pathos, and faith. The audience dissolved into heartful applause. That was the Kelly Niles I was able to know and treasure as a friend once I had left my reactivity behind.

Teachings Along the Way

Recently in India, I cut my foot and it got infected. It swelled and became hot and tender to the touch. At the same time I had contracted amoebic dysentery, so there was much pain in my stomach. One morning, alone in a hotel, getting out of bed and attempting to hop to the bathroom to try to relieve the pain in my gut, I tripped, fell, and cut the other leg.

I lay there, bleeding, hurting, angry at myself, frustrated, and filled with self-pity. At that moment all I wanted was to get out of my body completely. I wanted to be taken care of, too. After three or four minutes of wallowing in these highly emotional mind states, I awakened to my predicament and started to laugh. The whole situation had turned into a Grade B movie, with me in the leading role. But at the same moment, now as a witness of this rather dull film, I saw that when I was "in" my drama it really hurt psychologically as well as physically.

Once I reawakened, the hurt just became fun to play with. I thought of how uncompassionate I was to other people's suffering and how arrogant I was about "letting it go." Later that day, talking by phone to a woman in America who was dying, I apologized for how callous I had become to her pain, how glib I was in my advice for how she should deal with it.

I can see how my own pain engages me and teaches me, and, in relation to that, I can see how much I distance myself from others' pain and thus don't really allow them into my being. Usually I have enough control of the situation to keep that distance, but with my family, over recent years, it has been a different matter.

In 1985 I went to Burma with the intention of meditating for three months. At the monastery where I was practicing, the days followed one another in such simplicity and increasing subtlety of mind. I awoke at 3:00 A.M., washed, and was back in my cell beginning the first meditation sitting by 3:15. From then until 11:00 P.M., with only six interruptions, in an alternating sequence, I sat an hour, then did walking meditation for an hour. No books, no telephone, no newspapers, no conversation, no letters to write or read.

The interruptions consisted of two meals, at 6:00 A.M. and 11:30 A.M., an early afternoon nap, an interview with the Sayadaw (teacher), sometimes an evening discourse, and a few minutes for laundry. Yet, despite the absence of external excitement, each day was full to overflowing with my thoughts. My mind filled all the space and invested the trivia of the situation with great import:

how many flies had the spider at the window caught in its web and mummified, why was the cow down in the pasture lowing so plaintively, should I carry my umbrella to lunch, the new yogi three doors down looked sickly. And, perhaps the trivia of most significance, counting out the four M&M's (two peanut, two plain) that I took after lunch, just before the noon fast, as my reward for being "good."

And what was the purpose of this self-imposed, impoverished imprisonment, you might ask. The purpose was to deepen *samadhi,* or concentration, so that my awareness might be able to remain at rest, focused on one point, rather than being at the mercy of each sense stimulus or thought that arose. After I had been at the monastery for two months, the mind was truly quieting. I had seemingly exhausted every possible fantasy, remembrance, and plan. I was able to penetrate more deeply into the nature of phenomena and to bring to this examination clear awareness. I was filled with such peace and joy.

Then a cable arrived. It was from Phyllis, my stepmother. "I am sorry to disturb your meditation. I am being operated on for cancer on Tuesday. I thought you should know. Love, Phyl."

Phyl had married Dad when she was fifty-eight and he seventy-two. She was incredibly strong and healthy, and I had been delighted to welcome her into the family. She would look after Dad, and I would be relieved of some of the responsibility for him. I had felt that responsibility ever since my mother's death. Almost the last thing my mother had said to me was, "Take care of Dad." I had said I thought he could take care of himself, but she didn't agree. I didn't really understand what that death-bed request meant, but, whatever, I was happy Phyllis was around to help Dad. And now she was the sick one.

By then I was so conditioned to watch my mind that I observed how calm I remained in the face of this news. At the same time, I could feel myself revving up, mobilizing for action. Tuesday was only five days away, and I was halfway around the world. As the list of actions required formed itself in my mind, the first order of business was to advise the Sayadaw. Telegram in hand, I went up to his rooms, requested a special interview, waited for the translator to arrive, and presented the message.

In the silence following the reading of the telegram, the Sayadaw studied me closely. Then he said, "Don't go! You are arriving at a very important stage of your practice. You should not disrupt it now."

In reaction to his response, my mind kept repeating, Don't go? Don't go? How could I not go? All of my cultural training created the sense that of course I would go. I said, "I must go. My family needs me."

Another silence, after which the Sayadaw said, "You have the potential to train and free your mind so that you could truly relieve much suffering for many. If you go now in response to this call, you will forgo much of the progress you have made but which is not yet stabilized." In all of these comments, the Sayadaw's tone of voice showed that he understood and felt compassion and that he was simply stating the obvious.

At that moment the predicament presented itself with crystal clarity. A scale: on one side my genuinely altruistic aspiration for an enlightenment that could serve all beings and on the other my identity as my parents' child and as a member of a family, with all the expectations that went with that. The situation brought home to me the wisdom of the rituals for *sadhus* (spiritual seekers) and monks and nuns, a funeral in which they and their families acknowledge that their children have died to their membership in the family in order to pursue without conflict the spiritual path. But my family and I had no such understanding. And I could hardly change the rules in midstream, especially a stream in spate.

"I must go," I repeated.

The Sayadaw said, "If you were a Burmese I would insist you stay. But you are from another culture and I understand your decision. I'm sorry." A great wave of sadness swept over me. I was sorry too.

We looked at each other, and it was as if my karmic predicament flashed before my eyes: who I thought I was; how I had become that thought enmeshed in a web of expectations; how it all worked; and the sadness of the human condition. And that it was all right, just as it should be.

The peace stayed with me through airports and intensive care wards, where one finds precious little peace. I talked with doctors and nurses and my father—all of whom seemed deeply in need of just the quiet equanimity I could offer. Now I was becoming Hanuman, learning to serve. Equanimity is a valuable quality, but I sensed that there was far more than equanimity that I could offer to others. Some day I might be able to provide loving compassion as well. That, however, would be available only when my heart stayed open in the presence of the suffering of others, when my heart was breaking and I'd still have equanimity.

I didn't anticipate at the time that Phyllis's illness was to serve as the catalyst for awakening that compassion. I moved into Dad and Phyllis's home to help care for Phyllis during the next six months, during which her cancer metastasized, she underwent yet another operation, and finally she died. The whole period awakened incredible anguish within me. Dad was eighty-eight and had become increasingly quiet. Phyllis and I had been pretty close, as close as two stubborn old-time bachelors could be. She was really the only member of the family who showed any genuine personal interest in my spiritual life, and we had reflected about her experiences as a Christian. Now her illness and Dad's psychological absence cast us close together in a new way. She asked me to share all the decisions about her sickness and its treatment. And, in the course of doing just this, I became deeply attached to her. With my increasing attachment came the yearning for her to live and the fear of losing her.

After the needle biopsy of the spot that a CAT scan had shown in her liver, we were both on the phone to get the results. I was in my room looking at a picture of Maharajji. As we waited for the doctor to come on the line, I found myself saying to the picture, "If it's all the same to you, would you make the spot benign?" I was praying.

Then the doctor was there with his professional-kind voice saying, "I'm sorry, Mrs. Alpert, but the biopsy showed malignancy of the most virulent kind." I felt my heart harden and turn cold, and with true vehemence I spat out at my guru, "You son of a bitch!" A moment later my heart was flooded with warm love. I felt as if I was being held with the tenderest love. The sadness and pain at the imminent loss of my new friend Phyllis were no less, but the harsh, isolating, bitter anger was gone.

After the biopsy the surgeons pushed for another operation to remove a portion of Phyllis's liver. She didn't want the operation. I called specialists around the country. Surgery was the best option within allopathic medicine, but its chance of success was only about 20 percent. I didn't want Phyl to undergo the surgery, but I also didn't want to close the door. She was not open enough to alternative therapies, nor could I really advocate, with any real faith, any of them. Philippine psychosurgery, wheatgrass and coffee enemas, laetrile, macrobiotics, and so on: the scientist in me found little solace in the data most of these systems put forth.

It is probably true that if the patient has sufficient faith, any treatment works some of the time. But where was such faith to come from? Phyllis had grown up with Western medicine, and my faith was not strong enough to inspire her. In addition, I could see that Phyllis wanted to die so she wouldn't cause us any more trouble. Her deep inadequacy, which gave her a feeling that she had no right to exist, was in evidence. So the surgeon invaded her body once again, though Phyl and I both felt we were doing it because we didn't have the courage of our convictions.

A few months later, when we visited the surgeon's office for more test results, we sat together in the waiting room with the long-suffering patients with haunted eyes and frightened hearts who inhabit such a place. Then we were in the surgeon's private office, which had pictures of his wife, who had been an old flame of mine in high school days, and he was saying, "The cancer is all through your body. There is nothing more I can do."

Later Phyllis and I compared notes and discovered that we had both felt great compassion for the doctor. Here was the medicine man who could not make good the promise that seduced his patients into trusting his judgment, wisdom, and skill, and undergoing more and more suffering. In his zeal, he had oversold his product once again to make his patients and himself feel good. We saw him as an unfortunate victim of a system in which truth is bargained for some transitory solace that is no real comfort at all.

After that, Phyl and I turned our attention to the process of dying. I often lay on the bed holding her in my arms as we spoke softly and wonderingly of spirit freeing itself from the confines of such a sick body. Phyllis had been a fighter, a toughie, and she was often angry and depressed, petulant and in much pain. She and I collaborated in assessing how much pain medication she needed to reduce her pain and still keep her consciousness clear.

A few days before her death, something happened to Phyllis. She gave up. I felt her monumental struggle to control events just let go. The Phyllis with her familiar prickly personality was gone, but what emerged in its place was awesome. I felt as if I were witness to a chrysalis becoming a radiant butterfly. There was still pain, but it no longer seemed relevant. We spoke, but I felt her whispers coming from a peaceful place. Finally she was not fighting either life or death.

When the end came, she said to me with an authority that was unmistakable, "Sit me up." I put her legs over the edge of the bed and raised her body. One hand I placed on her chest, the other on her back to keep her body erect. Her head kept falling forward and back, so I put my head against hers to steady it. Then she took a large breath and expelled it, then inhaled a second time and again exhaled—much longer and slower than the previous one. And then the final third breath, inhaled and expelled—and then she was no more. Those of us who had been caring for her gathered at the bed and all felt as if she was blessing us at the moment of her departure.

Phyl's death engaged my heart, and, as a result, I saw that I *could* let down the walls that protected me from my own humanity. I needn't be so afraid of heartbreak. It would happen again and again as I let myself acknowledge that I was part of the family of all living beings, with all its joy and sadness. However, now I could see that the heartbreak and grief did not really separate me from the spiritual dimension in which I experienced spacious peace that appreciated the universe as it is.

Dad, as well as Phyllis, had lessons to teach about being human. By the time Phyllis died—the second wife Dad had lost to cancer—Dad had withdrawn even more deeply into himself. It wasn't that he seemed depressed. It was rather that he didn't find the physical plane very interesting. And with each increment of letting go, he seemed more and more content.

His speech almost disappeared. We had grown accustomed to hearing him say "There we are!" after completing some task such as sitting down or finishing his food. These were comforting words, the way he said them to himself and to us. That expression came to characterize for me something very deep. When Dad had begun to lose strength several years earlier, I'd decided to make my home the basement apartment in Dad and Phyllis's house. I traveled a good deal, but I could oversee the household affairs and make sure the two of them were safe and properly supported.

An incredible fellow, Ken Shapiro, had arrived right before Phyllis took sick and stayed until Dad's death, serving the family with a devotion and patience that awed me. He was only twenty-eight years old, yet content, day in, day out, year in, year out, to shop and cook and attend to Dad and sit quietly with him. Ken had come onto the scene because he found himself crying while reading the stories about Maharajji in *Miracle of Love*. He had come to make contact with someone who had been with Maharajji. His manner of arrival, his being available just when we needed him, his devotion to his work, and his dependability led me to feel that he was a gift from Maharajji—a perfect gift.

This period of looking after Dad's household gave me a profound sense of well-being for having the opportunity to serve my father. When Mother had been ill and dying, there was Dad to look after her—and, besides, I was far too busy being an independent, self-important somebody to find time or even acknowledge any responsibility for her care. Those were my years for slaying Dragons, capturing the Chalice, saving the World.

But now, as Dad aged, I too was aging, and my passions were quieting enough that I could penetrate more deeply into the rhythms of life. I sensed the error of my own culture in casting off the extended family, with its emotional safety net and filial duty. Having lived in the villages of India, I saw the way in which fulfilling family roles help give a form and meaning to life. But it was only as I acknowledged and fulfilled my duty to help make my father's final years secure and happy that I truly understood this. It made the cycles of generations harmonious. Dad's expression "There we are" said it all.

I had so often guided people to look right in front of them to find ways to serve, yet my "service" had taken me to the farthest reaches of the earth. Was that service more glamorous, more important, more appropriate? When service to my parents was finally added in, it somehow made all the service seem right. I was doing what was immediately before my eyes—the care of Dad—yet at the same time I was discovering an awakening compassion for all beings.

As good as it felt, I wasn't above milking it. When a member of the family commented on how good I was to be giving up my freedom to look after Dad, I looked slightly long-suffering and said, "Well, someone has to do it." In truth, my dealings with Dad and Phyllis over those years and through their deaths were a great enriching of my life, and the opportunity to take care of them was one I guarded jealously.

I was fortunate in that there were sufficient resources for us to maintain a large house that provided privacy when I needed it and enough money for full-time care that enabled me to come and go as my work required. But even with such support on the material plane, being with one's parents in later life is often difficult. They have become set in their ways, their interests are not necessarily your own, and they know just how to "get to you," to awaken whatever residual infantile guilt or inadequacy may be lurking in you. So unless you really want to work at using the sticking places within yourself as stuff worthy of your attention, it can be very difficult.

More and more, when the opportunity permits, we tend to surround ourselves with people who don't shake our inner applecart. They are often people who share our values, appreciate us, and leave us untroubled by the presence of our old habits, prejudices, opinions, and preferences. What are called the "uncooked seeds"—the seeds of aversions and attachments that lie dormant until the right circumstance provides the catalytic conditions for them to bloom and flower—are ignored. But I was pulled by a yearning to be liberated from all the clingings of my mind. So I sought out environments that were "hot fires"—that is, where the conditions were optimum for exposing those uncooked seeds.

Being in Dad's household as a fifty-five-year-old son named Richard certainly did expose those seeds. During the years I spent there, I had a chance to see, examine, and often transcend anger, boredom, self-righteousness, avoidance, and a patronizing attitude. At first it was, "Look at me, look what a good son I am." Then it was, "Doing this is good for me." Then there was, "Doing it efficiently." And finally there was, "Just doing it." In that setting I didn't quite arrive at the state of, "He does nothing and nothing is left undone," but it was getting closer.

Part of the wonder was in meeting Dad in continually new ways. In the shower washing his genitals, which had spawned me, changing his diaper as he had once changed mine, entering into his memory rooms as he repeated for the umpteenth time a conversation he had had in the

1920s—as if it were now and I were somebody else: his brother or his secretary or an important judge. And then there were the quiet moments in which we held hands and were silent watching the changing light and just sharing presence and now and then a squeeze of the hand. Such silence I had never known with Dad. We had always filled all the space in our family.

This very Buddhalike smiling silence, which showed a new and wonderful facet of Dad, was immensely upsetting to others. One member of the family, who had had difficulty getting along with Dad, interpreted Dad's silence as "He hasn't changed a bit. He still ignores me." And for Dad's adoring sister, his silence in response to her attempts to chat awakened the cry "Oh, Georgie, Georgie, what have they done to you? Oh, he's gone, he's gone!" Both of them suffered as they clung to outdated models of Dad. But Dad and I, gently holding hands in the present moment, couldn't have been happier. He died peacefully. For me, helping Dad feel safe in his frailty and death, as he had made me feel safe in my vulnerable infancy, was a completion. In the process, having an opportunity to bring to light and release so many old habits and posturings was "frosting on the cake."

When people are dying they often feel alone in their pain and fear. Those around them are not going through what they are, so how could they understand? It takes a lover who is not afraid of the pain to be present and wipe away the loneliness.

For over twenty-five years I have been often in the company of dying people. In the course of all those moments I have come to see just how in love I can stay with other beings in the face of their suffering. If I am afraid of pain, then in a subtle and sometimes not-so-subtle way I distance my heart from the dying person with whom I am sitting. If I am afraid of dying, then the very dying process of another awakens my fear and inevitably I push that person away so I can remain safe in my own "not dying" illusion. And if I am able to stay open to pain and even to dying but am afraid of the mystery of death itself, then at that final moment I will pull back from merging with the beloved, whose form is undergoing profound transformation.

Working with people with AIDS has offered me intensely deep experiences of my own holding and letting go. In the abstract, the thought of a person who is HIV positive and has AIDS symptoms opens my heart. The ones I have worked with have acquired their illness through being human, one way or another. I have had homosexual encounters and at one time shared needles. And so there, but for grace, go I.

As I start to open to each of these people, to his or her feelings of social ostracism, falling through the air with no economic net, dealing with the body becoming ugly, weak, painful, undependable because of the opportunistic nature of the illness—how far do I open? Who is this before me? Is this us in love to whom this is happening, or is it the safe distancing and a part of myself isolated as "him" or "her"? Each time I work with my reactions of closing down, of distancing myself from the "distressing disguise" of my guru, of my beloved, I see myself having once again "forgotten into fear." I flicker.

I sit with the situation. I quiet my mind while holding a hand or just sitting by a bed. I go deeper within myself,

far behind my identification and fears, back into awareness, mindful of our predicament but no longer lost in it.
The humanity is there, but so, too, is the spacious awareness. I have come into love, and I feel the barriers between me and this other being dissolve. I am with the
fear and the pain. With it yet simultaneously behind it.
We are together entering into the cave where we are no
longer alone in our suffering but behind and within it.

Learning to be open in the presence of dying is different from remaining open in the presence of death. With
each new opportunity to be with people as they die, with
my friends Carlos and Kenny, Bill and Sean, Ginny and
Jean, Lionel and Kate, and so many more, I come closer
and closer to staying open with the beloved through death
itself. Maharajji died in 1973. Our love stayed alive
through the barrier of death. The way in which our timeless love has transcended death makes me strong. Less
and less am I intimidated by the intensity of the death
process itself. It is just another shift in the ever-changing
panorama wrought by time.

The Seva Lessons

In late 1978, a door opened for me into a rich field for deepening compassion. Larry and Girija Brilliant, who were also devotees of Maharajji, invited me to a meeting in Ann Arbor, Michigan, for the purpose of starting a nonprofit organization dedicated to the alleviation of suffering in the world. I agreed to attend, even though I knew very little about the other invitees. I had been looking for ways to participate in larger-scale service opportunities than the one-on-one with which I was most familiar. And I was seeking a way to cultivate my relationships with peers. On both counts this seemed like a great opportunity.

At the first meeting at a conference center in the December snows of Michigan, I found a very mixed and confusing collection of people. For example, just before the meeting began, I found sitting opposite me a doctor from Washington wearing a three-piece suit and tie, with his dispatch case open before him. So, I thought, it's going to be that kind of a meeting. But then another person sat down next to the first man. This fellow wore a flamboyant sweatshirt and had wild hair, atop of which was a Day-Glo beanie with a propeller on it turning gently. Apparently it wasn't going to be "that kind of a meeting" after all. But my confusion at this strange duo was as nothing compared with that on the face of the Washington doctor as he became aware of and turned to acknowledge the fellow next to him. What could these two possibly have in common?

We were snowed in at our meeting for several days— and it took that long for us to get over our reactivity to one another and recognize that we shared a common desire to help relieve the suffering of the poor, sick, and disenfranchised of the earth. While this desire in me had found expression in small projects and personal encounters, many of the other participants came from the public health domain and had been able to help vast numbers of people.

For example, a core of the group had served together under the banner of the United Nations World Health Organization in the program to eradicate smallpox. No small undertaking, it had required the collaboration of thirty-five countries, and some two billion house calls, and the latest technology in vaccinations, information accrual, and logistical analysis, as well as incredible determination rooted in the faith that such an objective was realizable. These were seasoned veterans of a highly successful campaign. Many of us recall, only too well, our vaccinations and vaccination cards. It boggles the mind to realize that you don't have to be vaccinated for small-pox anymore, because there is none left anywhere in the world. Smallpox is the only endemic disease transmitted from person to person that has ever been eradicated from the face of the earth. Many of these women and men among whom I sat had such sophistication about the nature and causes of world suffering, such highly evolved technical skills, and such a sense of camaraderie that I was in awe. These were the big players, the adults in the world of the alleviation of suffering. What I was doing there I could hardly imagine, but, however I'd gotten there, I was definitely going to hang on.

The organization was to be called *Seva,* a Sanskrit word that translates as "service" (with a karma yoga connota-tion). *Seva* was also, however, an acronym for the Society for Epidemiological and Voluntary Assistance—a far more palatable meaning of the word for our compatriot with the dispatch case.

When the question arose as to which suffering we wanted to address, the medical and public health folks, who made up a disproportionately large percentage of the participants, proposed a variety of major public health projects. But one of these people, a French-Swiss doctor named Nicole Grasset, was strongly championing our taking on a campaign to eradicate preventable and cur-able blindness. She had recently been with Sir John Wil-son, a blind Englishman who headed the Commonwealth Society of the Blind, and he had explained that 80 per-cent of world blindness, representing some 20 million people, was preventable or curable. Nicole, who had led

the Southeast Asia team in the smallpox eradication program, was an attractive and charismatic woman, greatly
admired by her colleagues. I could imagine her in her
high heels and tasteful attire, cigarette in hand and little
dog under her arm, tirelessly leading a vast international
medical effort. She was convinced we should "take on"
blindness.

Now I had no particular brief for blindness in the
catalog of sufferings. Because I had focused so much on
the spiritual root cause of suffering—ignorance—and the
psychological sufferings of neurosis over the years, I felt
there was no way to assess which form of physical suffering was most worthy of attention. Childhood diarrhea,
hunger, poverty, ecological pollution, nuclear war? Each
was a major cause of suffering, real or potential. Because
my doctorate was in psychology and not medicine, other
than feeling sorrow for people, giving money to people
begging and checks to various agencies servicing those in
need of help, I had never attempted to intervene directly
in the world of physical suffering.

While I didn't quite understand what was involved,
I supported a blindness project as Seva's first endeavor.
What happened in the next few years amazed me. Nepal, which had many blind people and few facilities,
invited our group into their country to help. The Seva
Foundation was not an official NGO (nongovernmental
organization) in Nepal, but we were able to function
initially under the banner of the World Health Organization.

Our sophisticated team realized that before you can
solve a problem, you have to know its nature and dimen-
sions. So a huge survey was undertaken—complete with

trekking investigative teams, a helicopter, computers, and many staff members, expatriate volunteers, and Nepalese. By the completion of the survey, it was clear that while there were some childhood eye problems, by far the majority of the cases of blindness were caused by cataract. To bring back sight to a cataract-blind person requires an operation, often lasting only about four minutes, in which the outer cornea is cut, the opaque lens extracted, and the cornea stitched. After recuperation, the patient is given those thick, Coke bottle–like glasses and can see reasonably well. There was calculated to be a backlog of 200,000 cataract blind. Just thinking about being a blind person trying to survive in rocky, hilly terrain such as Nepal's, one of the poorest countries in the world, engaged my heart. Two hundred thousand such people became a numbing abstraction.

I was awed that we were going to attempt to take on this problem and help Nepal get rid of its huge backlog of cataract blind. I could play no part in the actual work in Nepal, being not an ophthalmologist, epidemiologist, or public health administrator. What I could do was raise funds. So that's what I did. We estimated that in the eye camps where the surgery was performed, often by flashlight in a temporarily converted schoolroom, the operation cost five dollars (it's now thirty dollars). From a fund-raising point of view, such a statistic was dynamite. Five dollars gave sight to a fellow human being or bought you a ticket to a movie. Wavy Gravy, the board member with the propeller beanie, ran rock-and-roll-music Eye Balls and benefits, and I gave lectures. We all wore T-shirts with the famous Buddha eyes of Nepal and the inscription "A solution in sight."

Sitting in on the meetings, I was learning an immense amount about how you undertake a venture of this magnitude. We involved other governments and charities, helped the Nepalese set up programs at every level. Within a few years we had come out from under the umbrella of WHO, and Seva was an NGO in its own right. There was a steady stream of volunteer ophthalmic surgeons we were enrolling and sending to Nepal. The politics of Nepal, a monarchy, was strange and delicate to work with, everything being at the pleasure of the king and queen.

It was also fun to explore spiritual issues with the group. For example, we came to one of our early meetings with $104,000 in our account. The cost of the projects we wanted to carry out, plus our overhead to date, was $96,000. The question we asked ourselves was whether committing that much of our capital, leaving us with so little to run on, was an act of faith or an act of irresponsibility. Despite the immense sense of responsibility reflected in this particular group, we opted to think of it as a matter of faith, voting to go ahead with the $96,000 commitment; then we stopped for dinner. Imagine what it did to our heads when, halfway through dinner, the telephone rang and it was one of our new friends, who said that he was very impressed with the coming together of skillful means and spiritual awareness in our organization and was donating $100,000.

The dynamics of our Seva family proved to be very intense. From early on we instituted a process called circle sharing, in which we went around the circle sharing our truths with one another. It wasn't always easy. In the course of so much activity, it was inevitable that toes would be stepped on, feelings hurt, and differences in ideologies become apparent. We attempted to bring these to light in order to become welded into a strong and dynamic unified heart, which would generate its own power.

It soon became apparent that there were some fundamental differences in life strategies. One of these came to be characterized as the difference between do-ers and be-ers. Many of the group had a long history of social action and service. They forged ahead to get things done, their goal being the eradication of the backlog of blind. They were the do-ers. I, and a few like me, in contrast, felt that *how* we did the work was more important, that the means and the ends were of a piece. To be too focused on your goal or objective could lead you to act in ways that created other suffering even as you were alleviating some. We were the be-ers, advocating that we move only at a rate at which we could remain awake as we acted.

We had set as our objective eradicating the backlog of cataract blind in Nepal in five years. Realizing that objective in a world of bureaucratic inertia meant pushing pretty hard against a great many people and their vested interests. It meant ruffling a lot of feathers.

In the sixties and early seventies, I had watched how the anti–Vietnam War movement, motivated as it was by concern for human life and by a growing understanding that the United States operates for economic and geopolitical gain as well as from moral principles and national defense, created a cultural backlash. I saw that, as in former times, the combination of righteousness and immaturity untempered by sufficient wisdom can do real violence. If we wanted only to wipe away the backlog, then any means, fair or foul, was acceptable. But if we were interested in a reduction of overall suffering in the world, then the means must be carefully attended to.

In contrast to many members of the group, I realized how extreme my position had become. I focused so much on the process of living, on the quality of be-ing from moment to moment, that the product often emerged very slowly and sometimes got entirely lost in the shuffle. When I perceived that an objective might require pushing against someone, exerting power over another person to get what I wanted, I often gave up rather than confront others or find another way to resolve the problem.

Looking back to the prepsychedelic times, when I was preoccupied with my own need for love and approval, I see the double bind that need placed me in. To gain the approval of my superiors and parents, I was called to extraordinary feats of achievement. For example, in 1961 I was holding posts in four separate departments at Harvard as well as a research appointment at Stanford. In order to keep "Sammy" running at such incredible levels of productivity, I saw everyone except my superiors as objects to be manipulated to bring about the realization of my goals. Of course, I had to step on and over many people, who then disliked me. But that was a sacrifice I had to bear in order to offer the spoils of my achievement to my superiors, whose love and approval *really* counted.

When I awakened finally and saw just how I had separated myself from the human family, my behavior started to change. And it was still in transition eighteen years later when we—the do-ers and the be-ers—met head-on. In the intervening years I had reacted against the reprehensible upward climber that I had seen myself to be by attending more and more to the dynamics of each situation—the "heart" of the matter. Of course, the old me didn't die easily, and, during the seventies, I would revert to my old manipulative ways, then catch myself and drop them. In truth, I often got so lost in achieving (of course, it was my zeal to do good) that I couldn't independently catch myself. But people around me would begin to express the feeling that they didn't quite trust me. Those remarks would make me angry, and my anger would awaken me to the problem. I would realize that I was angry because there was truth in what they said. They had busted me, and after I got over the first feelings of fury and verbal attacks in retaliation, I had the good fortune (karma) to want to be free more than I wanted to be right. Then I could admit that I had gotten caught in old habits . . . again.

At one famous Seva board meeting, Nicole was clearly overworked and exhausted, frustrated and angry with many of her staff and the mercurial bureaucrats with whom she had to deal. I suggested that perhaps she was going about her work in a less-than-conscious way. The battle lines were drawn. I had just put myself in the ring as a be-er in the face of Nicole, unchallenged champion of the do-ers. At one point the dialogue got so heated that I recall Nicole saying that she was determined to do everything in her power not to let one blind person remain blind a day longer than necessary. I retorted that there were worse things than being blind and that she herself was suffering in her very acts to relieve suffering. Nicole reiterated that she didn't think that there were worse things than being blind and that, as far as she was concerned, she'd sell her own soul to bring sight to another individual.

It was a romantically dramatic and often quite acrimonious debate, which we all remember. In the course of it, we became aware that Nicole and I, in our extreme positions, were reflecting the very creative tensions of Seva itself. This continuing dialogue, if it did not rip us apart, could make us strong. And indeed it has, because I realized that I had gotten out of balance in focusing on means at the expense of goals, and Nicole in subsequent years tempered her behavior and started to use periods of quiet contemplation to gain balance in her own life.

At moments of our fiercest confrontation, I found myself quite ready to walk away from Seva. I couldn't get caught in our wishful mythologizing. If Seva was to be just another Western-style achievement mill, successful as it might be, I couldn't see a place for myself in it. For the first five or six years, I would get discouraged easily. In our zeal to meet our deadline, we would settle into safe and efficient roles with one another so as not to rock the boat. Then we would begin to hide our truths from one another. I so firmly believed that each truth hidden, no matter how trivial or potentially painful, put distance between people, and that if we aspired to function as one heart we had to live with one another in truth. It was still the same debate. Could we afford the time to truly "be" with one another?

Many years, in my discouragement that we were selling out, I would come to the meetings and announce rather melodramatically that I was going to resign from the board because it was no longer an "interesting enough organization." It was no longer keeping itself at the very edge of the exploration of living truth. I felt that if I was going to affiliate myself voluntarily with other people, I wanted to find *satsang*, that is, the company of people who are truly seekers after truth. I could not believe that truth and compassionate action need be at odds with each other.

The first few times I threatened to resign, my threat precipitated a paroxysm of group self-examination. Each time, I found by the end of the meeting that the embers of possibility were still bright in the organization, and when we came to the beautiful conclusion of the meeting, during which we would go around the circle and reaffirm our individual desire to remain in the group, I found myself affirming my commitment to Seva, often with considerable emotion.

But just as the person who cries "wolf" too often is ignored, I found after a few years that when I threatened to resign someone would say, "Here goes Ram Dass again." Finally, a few years ago, Larry said that I shouldn't do it anymore. The organization was now strong enough, and if I wanted to resign I should do so. He felt I needed Seva as much as Seva needed me.

He called my bluff, because nowhere did I know of another group of people who had come so far in their efforts to deliver high-quantity, high-quality, low-cost conscious and compassionate service to their fellow beings. There might have been organizations that either accomplished more or were able to be spiritually awake together more often, but none I could find had more successfully or creatively integrated spirit and action in a way that worked for me. This is not to imply that Seva is very far along either on this journey. Seva is only at the beginning. It is still full of contradictions, unconscious actions, fear, and institutional calcification and errors. But in the midst of all this, the living spark is truly there, and we recognize it, and still share the collective desire to fan it.

More and more each year, each of us has realized how much the ultimate success of our experiment is dependent upon the work we do on ourselves. We all have rich and engrossing lives independent of Seva, and it is not easy to choose to roast in the fire of truth when there are so many competing and less painful ways to spend our time and energies.

Over these years with the Seva family, another change has occurred in me. It has to do with control. After I came out from under the power of the neurosis in which I gave to my superiors and the powerful people so much control over me in my zeal to be loved, I reacted by keeping control myself. I just assumed that my own judgments were always the wisest. In Seva, however, I found that often my original opinions, attitudes, and certainties were tempered by the wisdom of the group. While there was no individual in the group whose opinion I could invariably trust more than my own, I found again and again the group's collective wisdom to be greater than my own. It was a new kind of trust I was experiencing, and one I valued. We find in our meetings that we are each privy to a little truth, but we also have the discriminative wisdom to cherish the greater truth, and sometimes even know it when we hear it.

At the end of five years (our initial deadline), not only had Nepal not become free from its backlog but there were not enough operations being performed to take care of the 25,000 new cases of cataract there each year. We were still losing ground, even though we had enlisted the active aid of many countries and moved well ahead in helping the Nepalese put in place an infrastructure to handle their own eye care.

Recognizing our failure to meet our deadline and considering the years it would take to realize our objectives was sobering indeed. I had come out of the more or less "hit-and-run" mentality so evident in the sixties. We would introduce something into the culture, and, if it didn't "take" in short order, we would simply conclude that we were ahead of our time, that the culture wasn't ready, and we'd drop it and try something else. For us, to "be here now" seemed to mean to remain light and uncommitted so that, when a situation was experienced as not enough or wanting, we could "let go lightly."

Seva was facing a long-term commitment—at least another seven to ten years. I saw that sustainability and perseverance over time were not qualities I had cultivated. I found in myself an aversion to being part of this commitment. Yet I saw quite clearly that, in order to honor our human contracts with the blind, with our staff, and with the dedicated Nepalese we had involved in our fantasy, a commitment would have to be made. It gave a new, richer, and more timeless meaning to "be here now."

As I write this, twelve years have passed since the Nepal blindness project began. The backlog of blind people awaiting surgery is being reduced, and the Nepalese have a strong and deep infrastructure in place for eye care.

The director of the U.S. National Eye Institute has declared the Nepal Eye Program the most successful eye program in the international field of work in developing countries. And our involvement is becoming less and less necessary.

We have, of course, received invitations to turn our attention to eye programs in other developing countries now that Nepal has come so far. In response to this obvious need and to our long-term objective of alleviating the world's blindness problems, we have recently been meeting at Aravind Eye Hospitals in Madurai (South India) to collaborate in the creation of an International Institute for Community Ophthalmology. Here, teams from developing countries around the world will be invited to share with Aravind, the Nepalese, and Seva the skills, strategies, and perspectives necessary to create programs in their own countries. A natural next step.

Having borne witness and participated in this amazing sequence of events, I find myself less skeptical about the possibility, championed by Dr. Venkataswamy of Aravind and by Nicole, that preventable and curable blindness in the world can be turned into a nonproblem. The Lions Club International has just given $20 million to the cause. Maybe the time is right and fair winds are blowing.

The Nepal Eye Program provided another lesson, which now serves me in good stead in understanding and articulating karma yoga as a viable spiritual path. I had joined Seva happy to raise funds and sit in the back of the bus. Thus, it was disconcerting one day to find myself chairperson of the board. According to our practice of one- or two-year terms, to have a continuously changing vision at the helm, it was inevitable—but still strange. I was not a particularly good chairperson. I left almost everything to Suzanne Gilbert, the executive director, and just signed a few papers and went on raising money. I think I was too uncomfortable in the role to take it seriously.

Everyone in Seva would say that it is good that I didn't take myself seriously, because we have a "thing" about that word. In fact, Wavy Gravy introduced a pair of Groucho Marx–like glasses to the board meetings. Anyone who uses the word *serious* is required to stop and put on the funny glasses. This ritual serves, as Wavy pointed out, to keep us from taking ourselves too seriously, a real danger in service organizations such as ours. As we deal with the horrendous sufferings in the world, Wavy often needs to remind us that "if you don't have a sense of humor, it just isn't funny."

As chairperson I visited our program in Nepal. There were a number of ongoing projects that required some board member involvement, and that year I was chosen to go. I had been thrown out of Harvard in 1963, and now, twenty years later, the act of putting on a blue blazer and striped tie and representing an institution in the official world was bound to reawaken old habits. I would have to be Dr. Dass.

In Nepal I found it necessary to visit a government official to bargain for some relaxation of bureaucratic red tape. In return I was authorized to sweeten the pot somewhat. So we met: he with his entourage, me with mine. We had tea and made small talk prior to getting down to business. I was very uptight because I realized that I had to be an astute bargainer, and my tie, literally and symbolically, felt too tight. I was back into my old mode of twenty years ago, seeing the man as a bureaucratic object to be manipulated for my own ends. My counterpart, by contrast, was doing his best to understand a chairperson of an American foundation (and in his mind all American foundations were like wish-granting trees or geese that lay golden eggs), who was called Ram Dass and was holding a *mala* (beads).

Just before we were to begin the serious part of the meeting, I looked up in my nervous state and found him looking at me. Our eyes met and held. There, behind the government ministerial role, was another being, just like me. At that moment I felt great joy as his gaze released me from imprisonment in my role as chairperson. We were two beings about to enter into a formal, stately, and highly ritualistic dance together, or perhaps we were about to start a game of Monopoly, and Government Minister was the top hat piece; Chairperson was the thimble or iron.

In that situation, my government friend, as a truly spiritual Easterner, was not caught in his role. And his seeing behind his role allowed me to stop being entrapped in my own. So often in subsequent years I have remembered that instant, and the memory of it awakens me again to the entrapment of the moment and helps me to dance free. And often now I find myself in the role of the "eyes," inviting another being, in the midst of a seductive drama, to come out and play.

Visiting Guatemala to work on our projects there taught me other valuable lessons about compassion. We were visiting the villages where Seva's goat and sheep projects were under way. These communities are composed mostly of women, young children, and a very few men. The women had watched their husbands, sons, and parents killed before their eyes. Later those who did not cross to Mexico returned to their villages, in which buildings had been ransacked and burned, animals killed, crops destroyed. There was nothing left, and still they held on. They reminded me of the tiny blue flowers one finds growing in rock crevices high above the tree line, seemingly out of the rock itself. They are buffeted by winds, nourished by so little, and still they hang on.

Seva, in alliance with a Guatemalan NGO, had provided goats and sheep to give these women and their children, who were not really strong enough to replace the men at growing corn, their source of food and livelihood. And when we visited villages to which the animals had been given only a few short years before, we found that the project was working. The children were healthy from the goat milk, there was meat and a little money from the sale of baby goats and sheep. What we hadn't expected, however, was that these bumptious animals, which the women and older children held on ropes to display to us, brought them more than physical survival. They brought laughter and joy.

How different these villages were from the ones we visited the next day, villages that hadn't yet begun a project, where there was still nothing . . . nothing. The people met with us and explained that they had no seed, no hoes, no water; all they had was their will to work if we would only loan them enough to get started.

There were thirteen such villages, and, no matter

how we tried to juggle the Seva funds, there would be enough to help only four of them in the next fiscal year. We explained this to the Mayans. Our inability to help weighed heavily on us, because we could see how many of these people would die as a result. I don't recall ever experiencing so powerfully that link between funds raised at lectures and benefits and the preservation of life itself.

The Mayans' response to our offer was an interesting one. They said that the funds we could provide to the four villages they would divide among the thirteen. We weren't happy, because so little funding per village might not be sufficient to assure life for everyone, and we told them that. Their reply remains with me now. "From our holy book, the *Popul Vuh,* we have learned that when you are walking along together and one person falls, you help that person up, and then everyone walks just a little bit slower." Their words spoke of what a real sense of family is about. We went back to North America and raised the rest of the money.

Besides these field expeditions, and meeting around the circle, we at Seva meet often on the volleyball court, where some of the most retiring of us suddenly turn into animals who smash the ball down in the opponents' court and laugh gleefully. Or we meet in sweat lodges, where one or another of us prays in a way that touches deeply, or at a Grateful Dead concert, where we join in celebrating that religious ritual. We spend time with the many children the group has spawned and with our Nepalese, East Indian, Guatemalan, and Native American friends who come to our meetings. We travel together, bumping along in jeeps in remote corners of the globe or work together on one project or another. Finally, I have come to appreciate living among peers. We are so different, yet over the years our mutual love and respect have become strong. We listen to one another, we bust one another when we get too phony, and we enjoy one another. No one misses meetings if she or he possibly can help it.

Readiness

Maharajji's injunction that I "be like Gandhi" has led me to work with many of Gandhi's quotations.

Gandhi was once on a train that was about to pull out of a station. A reporter rushed up to the train window and requested a message from Gandhi that he could take back to his village. As the train began to move, Gandhi handed him a sentence that he had hastily scribbled on a piece of paper bag: "My life is my message."

Intuitively I feel the truth of that statement for each of us. Our relations with one another are ultimately rooted in what we are, in what all of our experiences, education, and karma have made us. That quotation causes me to examine my activities, not in a self-conscious way but rather as a source of clues to the ways in which I am not living with integrity. For the past thirty years I have been trying to integrate into my life what I learned in 1961.

The disparity between what we know and how we act has always irritated me and goaded me onward.

One evening in the early seventies, I recall driving out of the parking lot of the Berkeley Community Theater, where I had just given a lecture. It was a cold night, and I was in a line of cars edging its way slowly forward. As my defroster, on full, cleared the windshield and the heater blew only cold air, I saw that the car in front of me was one of those deliciously ugly early VW vans. On the back window were stickers proclaiming WE ARE ALL ONE, LOVE IS THE WAY, and even one that said, BE HERE NOW.

I felt happy. Waves of love came from my romantic heart toward these gentle hippies in front of me, who were obviously awakening to the deeper truths and harmonies of the universe. As I was luxuriating in our flower children—ness, I saw the driver's side window open and an object thrown out. Through the window I heard the music and words of John Lennon's "Love, Sweet Love." What had been thrown out was a crumpled paper coffee cup. I was upset; my heart closed. These people weren't sensitive, caring flower children—they were mindless, uncaring clods who were soiling their own nest, littering their own living room.

The juxtaposition of the moments of open and closed heart showed me the mercurial nature of my own mind. At first, what I projected about them made me "us" with them. But a moment later, based on their one act, they became "them." How quickly I disassociated myself from what I found unpalatable. The people in the car had not yet integrated what their minds, and even perhaps their emotional hearts, knew with their actions. But have I been so integrated myself? I can recall so many times when who I said I was did not correspond to the way I acted. In each case I can see that the lack of correspondence was caused by my attachment to a model I held in my mind at the moment of who I *thought* I was and what I *thought* I should be doing. As a result, I was no longer present to the moment and listening.

Two instances come to mind, both of which happened in 1984 when I was house-sitting a farm in western Massachusetts and working on the book *How Can I Help?* with Paul Gorman. One day I ran out of typing paper in the middle of a creative writing surge and drove quickly to town to buy more. Along the way I passed a one-legged hitchhiker. And I didn't stop because I knew how long it would take him to get in and out of the car with his crutches. And I was obviously in too much of a rush writing *How Can I Help?* to stop.

At that time there were some renovations going on in the farmhouse, and a young carpenter was working in the basement. I was nervous about my writing and my deadline, so I deflected his efforts to visit with me. After a few days, he seemed agitated and asked if there was any time he could come by and talk with me. I explained that I was sorry but I was writing and could not be disturbed. He said he understood. Four days later he stuck a gun into his mouth and blew his brains out.

Recognizing the relationship between the different parts of my life, such as my faith in my own intuition and my dependability in dealings with others, has been important to me. There were times when the lack of integrity in my motives led me to make promises that later, when a different motive was dominant, I had no interest in fulfilling. Because of this, people close to me pointed out that I was untrustworthy. I defended myself against the charge, but later I saw that they were right. Over the years, however, as I have more fully integrated the disparate parts of my being, I find myself far more trustworthy in my dealings with others. It feels wonderful. This, of course, does not mean that I don't change direction from time to time, but now the changes are more timely, less violent, and more part of a deeper continuity in truth-wisdom.

I have learned to trust my intuition, and I've learned to do it sooner. It's taken a long time to realize that it isn't so important that I understand intellectually what I'm doing. More important is that I feel the validity of my action. That is the way I know that it fits in with the deeper harmonies of the universe. "I feel it intuitively" is heard by some as a weak and waffling response. I don't care. I'm not going to resist actions based on my intuition just because I can't justify them. I don't find my judgmental faculty nearly as wise as my intuitive one.

To integrate all the aspects of one's being certainly does not mean that there will be no tension. In fact, an integrated being is one who has within herself or himself many forces balanced in a creative tension. For example, I am a very gregarious person, perhaps even a people junkie. Despite my protests that I like to be alone, I keep organizing my life to be in the company of wall-to-wall people. The paradox is that when I am alone, after four or five days of mild depression, agitation, and a few rounds of self-pity and paranoia, I break out above the ego-smog and soar blissfully in the light of joy and equanimity.

I had thought of the spiritual journey as basically a loner journey for me. Maharajji had said, "Ram Dass should be alone much. He should not be with people so much." But shortly after he said that, he gave me a chastising glance for not being available to a couple who were having marital difficulties and wanted to talk with me. Little wonder I continued to experience these opposing pulls, and the tensions to which they give rise.

Over the past twenty years I have been alternating, or I prefer to think of it as "spiraling" upward, between these two modes. For a while I am playing in the marketplace of ignorance, which gives rise to greed and lust, hatred and ill will, agitation, sloth, and doubt. Over time in such an environment, my own clingings, aversions, fears, and desires begin to take form, to become "real." Sooner or later (and, with grace, it gets continually sooner), I realize I have become toxic again and am forgetting the deep truths that lie within my awareness. (What grace to even notice.)

I agree with Thomas Merton that if you yourself are drowning you cannot provide much in the way of assistance to another drowning person. Thus, with this justification, I have retreated into environments that remind me and call me back into a spiritual perspective. Once there, I see again the transitory and mind-generated quality of phenomena and I feel the peace of allowing the innate wisdom of the universe to manifest as it will. And then, after whatever time is necessary, I feel the pull to take up the tools of my trade and reenter the arena, the marketplace of tears and pleasures, to play my part.

As I approached my sixtieth year, I decided to take a

sabbatical from all service for a year. Another spiral! Perhaps I'd paint or travel or meditate. I wouldn't even plan it but rather would let it evolve. After I had made that decision, I was sitting with my elders in India, those devotees who spent years with Maharajji and who carry his spirit in their hearts and bones. When I presented my plan to them, there was silence. Then, simply but very definitely, one man whom I highly respect said in a most impersonal way, "That would be a mistake. I don't think Maharajji would want you to put off helping the suffering people now, in the hope that you might be able to do more later." What he said resonated deeply within me.

I knew he was delivering a message, and, at that moment, the idea of a sabbatical lost its power over me. He didn't leave it at that, however. He said, "If you feel the need to have quiet time and still do service, just get up earlier." Still spirals, but instead of year cycles, or months or weeks or even days, he was instructing me to reduce the cycles to hours.

I could see the handwriting on the wall. Sooner or later I would have to integrate these actions, not just live with creative tension. The stages of the spiritual journey were now coming more clearly into view. The awakening . . . then the withdrawal from the world to establish a spiritual base . . . and next the return to the world to integrate spirit and matter. First the spiraling as one goes sequentially from retreat to action out in the world and back into retreat again, and, finally, with integration, to a state of meditation in action.

For that final integration to occur, I would have to be able to be in every situation without my mind being entrapped by it. The only thing about being with people that "brings me down," that keeps me from resting in spacious awareness, that deflates that state of joyful equanimity, is my own mind: my own attachments or aversions, my own desires with regard to these people. If indeed I didn't *want* something—either from people or from their leaving me alone—I would be free and my joy and equanimity would not be disturbed even as I served.

I can see that I am not ready for that final integration. I am still too young—spiritually. This is not a new feeling for me. When one acts from the edge of one's capacities, that is often how one feels. But the imperative to act calls the tune. The Mayans—like my stepmother, Phyllis, and my father—are family. I can't turn away, and they can't wait. Action with faith is the only choice. It becomes the fire of purification.

That one will act is certain, but what action? I recognize readiness for some acts and not for others. Politics, for example, is an arena in which I feel I may have some role to play ("Be like Gandhi"), but I don't feel ready.

Being in Guatemala the first time awakened in me such a contradictory mélange of emotions. On the plane and in our hotel rooms we read and discussed books about the history of the situation. It was clear that it was the United Fruit Company in the fifties that had precipitated the present horror. A socially concerned government had offered to buy unused land in Guatemala from the huge U.S.-owned company to distribute among the peasants. The fruit company became concerned that the land reform might ultimately jeopardize their landholdings, and the wife of the head of United Fruit, who worked for President Eisenhower, convinced him to convince the secretary of state, John Foster Dulles, to convince *his* brother, Allen Dulles, head of the newly emerging CIA, to overthrow the government of Guatemala and install a military junta that would protect and represent the interests of the landed aristocracy. (About 4 percent of the population owned 85 percent of the land.) Now, many years later, we were still training the Guatemalan military elite in the States and backing a political regime in which human rights is a travesty.

Walking the streets in Chichicastenango, we were very aware of the military presence everywhere—soldiers in twos or threes with automatic guns at the ready patrolled the streets and markets. The weapons they carried were Israeli-made Uzis. As both an American and a Jew, I felt ashamed to be identified with people who could be witting parties to inflicting such suffering on others.

Of course, I had known that, historically, our U.S. national policies, so often singularly based on economic self-interest, had violated the human rights and lives of others. But I was one of the beneficiaries of these policies, one of the 6 percent of the world population using 40 to 50 percent of the natural resources, and I chose not to notice. But now I had to notice. The result of our policies was in the faces and hearts before my eyes. And I felt the deep stirrings of political indignation at myself and my people.

It was on this same trip that we visited the Mayan ruins of Palenque, deep in the jungle of Mexico. The silent stones and pillars speak of a time and a people of great spiritual power and dignity and wisdom. The long stairways, with their large, high steps, put the little human back into perspective. It made us feel like children navigating in an adult world. The imposing structures still standing also contributed to the feeling that we human beings are a part of a much vaster system, which lies shrouded in mystery.

I sit alone cross-legged in the portico of what remains of the Sun Temple, one of the many temples in the complex. I have come with Mira, Jai Lakshman, and Owen (Mira's son), mostly to see an architectural curiosity, a site from which one could imagine the evolved and advanced Mayan civilization that reached its height from A.D. 300 to 900.

We had just come from the refugee camps in Chiapas, where I found myself emotionally devastated by the conditions in which the three hundred Guatemalan refugees existed. These Mayans, though destitute, still retained their dignity, inner beauty, and connectedness to rhythms of the universe, remnants of their ancient heritage. They had fled Guatemala after the violence of the mideighties, when thousands of landless Mayan Indians had been killed or had just "disappeared" because they were considered a Communist threat. The only real threat, of course, was the suffering of the Mayans and their desire for themselves and their families to survive.

In the camps, the refugees lived in tin-roofed sheds with dirt floors, which became foot-deep mud in the rains. Water for 120 people came from one hose, and only the men who worked in the sugarcane fields, from which they returned soot-blackened by the burning of the cane, were allowed to wash. The children, even though their bone structure tended to hide it, were severely malnourished, their reddish, brittle hair attesting to vitamin deficiencies. These people had fled violence only to end up as slaves.

It's raining gently, as I sit in meditation, fog shrouding the ruins with a sense of mystery. As my meditation gets deeper, I feel that I am not alone. I open my eyes and look around, but no one is there. When I close my eyes, it's there again . . . the very strong feeling of presences. I tune to them, and I experience old beings surrounding me. I feel that I am in the presence of the Mayan elders. Are they actually present, or is it my imagination creating more melodrama? Are those actually different? Don't we know if anything's "out there" only through the workings of our minds anyway? I don't profess to know. All I have is the momentary experience. A great sadness washes over me as images of the destitute Mayans flash through my heart-mind. I find myself silently crying out before these elders, "How can I help?" The answer comes with a profound inner resonance that impresses itself deeply: "Tell your people." That is all.

It was only a few weeks later that I received a call from Holley Raven and Brian Willson. Brian is an extraordinary man who grew up in a working-class American family and found himself an officer in the service in Vietnam. He experienced a deep sense of revulsion at what we were doing and why. He became a leader of the opposition. A few years later when he saw firsthand the rows of young and old Nicaraguans with their legs ripped away by the land mines we were supplying to the Contras, he actively protested. It was on the railroad line outside the land mine factory in California, where he was protesting by sitting on the tracks, that the train didn't stop, intentionally, and Brian himself lost both legs.

Holley said the vote for aid to the Contras was coming up and there were to be protest rallies throughout the country, and would I speak. I was honored to be asked, because I was rarely invited to political gatherings. I explained that I had no firsthand knowledge of Nicaragua but had just returned from Guatemala. They pointed out that the protests were really about our outdated and inhumane policies in Central America and that I should speak whatever was in my heart.

My schedule had me moving around the country in a rather frenetic way for the following few weeks, and the only rally I could make was the one in Washington. So, only three weeks after leaving Guatemala, I found myself on the Capitol steps with Jacqueline Jackson, Jesse's wife, Amy Carter, Dan Ellsberg, and Brian Willson, and when the microphone was handed to me I found myself speaking of the great suffering and the great beauty of the Mayan people. And as I spoke I felt once again the presence of those elders. A vow so freshly made, so soon realized.

I see I am becoming politicized. The Mayan women are a part of me. They feel as though they are my family. And it is my words that are giving utterance to their pain. What is the tone of those words? Am I getting lost in the very emotions and the resultant acts that will polarize people and, in the long run, create more suffering? Or does my twenty years of spiritual work mean I can, like Gandhi, oppose in a way so as to unite? On the brink of letting myself into the hot waters surrounding the politics of justice, I wonder if I am evolved enough. Is it time yet for me to act in this way? Can I be in the presence of such agitation, righteous indignation, and condemnation and still retain the healing qualities I might contribute? In confronting injustice, can I keep alive my own equanimity, my appreciation for each person's karmic predicament, my love for all my fellow beings (though not necessarily for their actions), my ability to be in a situation of palpable fear without being consumed by the fear itself, and, simultaneously, my wisdom born of quietness?

There is one particularly startling afterimage to the Guatemala trip that brings home to me the matter of polarization and the pain it causes. At the end of our stay, I flew from Guatemala City to Los Angeles, where I had business. I was staying in Brentwood, a fashionable suburb west of Beverly Hills. As I drove my rented car down the quiet side street, I realized suddenly that I had entered a heavy mind space. There were no people on the tree-lined street, which was bordered on both sides by high walls. Behind the walls stood multimillion-dollar structures. Entrance to each home was via an electronic gate monitored by a video camera. On each neatly manicured strip of grass in front of the walls were red signs posted by the security company that obviously served this entire neighborhood. On each red sign, in bold black letters, the words ARMED RESPONSE.

I had just come from villages in the Guatemalan highlands where the poorest of the poor peasants cowered in fear of the military, who were in the service of the rich. And now, just a few hours later, I was in a village where the richest of the rich cower behind their security illusions, terrified of the poor—frightened enough to threaten bodily harm to protect, most likely, their insured possessions. The war between the haves and the have-nots is heating up. The disenfranchised of the world, label them what you will, are becoming too many, and the lack of compassion that this incredible discrepancy between rich and poor demonstrates is turning the world into frightened armed camps and great military bastions. This lack of compassion is an indictment of the ethics of governments and the successful and wealthy citizens that they represent. It is an indictment of all of us conspirators in what Thomas Berry calls "a dys-functional cosmology." And it ends up hurting all of our hearts.

Where do I stand amid these extremes, with my rented carriage house with fireplace and hot tub in the Marin hills? Where do I stand with my '74 Mercedes and '74 MGB and mountain bike? Where do I stand with my checking account and MasterCard, with my book and tape royalties, lecture and retreat fees?

Where are the homeless and poor and the suffering in this life-style? How much am I ready to hear? Maharajji slept in culverts under the roads, in fields, in the houses of rich and poor. It made no apparent difference. Maharajji cautioned me about money. He said, "Ram Dass should not touch money. Money should go around you, not through you." I am his disciple. But disciple of what teaching?

I've learned that if I try to divest myself of some attachment too soon, it just goes underground, biding its time, before surfacing again. The yogic literature cautions us not to attempt to rip the skin off the snake. We have to wait for the moment when the snake sheds its skin. If we do violence to ourselves in our zeal to get on with it, there are repercussions. Only when we are free from the attachments to our life-style, from the fear of losing it, will we know what components are appropriate to our unique expression of dharma. Until then, we must be gentle with ourselves, stay conscious of the relationship between our spiritual values and our life-styles, and make haste in our purifications slowly.

Love and Truth in Service

I had returned to India for the second time in 1971 but was unable to find Maharajji. He moved about a great deal and was not always so easy to locate. When I had exhausted the obvious possibilities, I decided to enroll with some friends in some meditation courses in Bodh Gaya, where the Buddha had become enlightened under the bodhi tree. I thought that if it had worked for him, it might work for me.

After almost forty days of practice, I felt the need for a change and decided to accept an invitation to a celebration in honor of Shiva that would be held in Delhi. A number of other Westerners who had been at the course decided to join me, and, boarding a friend's bus, we set out. The route to Delhi took us through Allahabad, a stately old city with wide, tree-lined thoroughfares and a fine university. Allahabad is best known for the Prayag:

the confluence of two of India's most sacred rivers, the Ganges and the Jamuna, with a third spiritual river, the Saraswati, rising from underground. For a Hindu, it is very auspicious to bathe where the rivers join, particularly at certain moments determined by the positions of the stars and planets. At these times, many millions of people come to Allahabad for the *mela*, a monthlong religious gathering during which people camp on the banks of the rivers and bathe at the appropriate moments.

When we arrived in Allahabad, one of these moments had just occurred. A member of our traveling group had been at the mela and suggested we make a small detour to where the rivers meet. It was already late in the afternoon on our first day out of meditation. We were all tired and still had some miles to go before arriving at our lodgings. I, as the elder in the group, opted that we not stop. But then I began to feel that that decision was not appropriate. After all, we were here on spiritual pilgrimage, and this spot was among the most sacred in India. A little fatigue should not deter us. I changed my mind and asked the driver to make the detour so that we could watch the sun set at the mela grounds.

When we arrived at the area, it was all but deserted: a vast, sandy campground with the river in the distance. The driver asked where he should park the bus. Dan, who had visited the mela and brought us small medallions of the deity Hanuman, suggested that we pull up near the Hanuman temple. Just as the bus was coming to a stop, Muffin, a two-year-old member of our party, shouted, "There's Maharajji."

Sure enough, Maharajji was walking with a companion just by the side of the bus. We all piled out and surrounded him, falling at his feet. Most of the group were seeing him for the first time. I was so overwhelmed by this "chance" meeting that I was holding on to his feet and crying uncontrollably.

After some time, Maharajji said something, and the man with him translated that Maharajji wanted us to follow him in our bus. Maharajji and the other man got into a bicycle rickshaw and started off down the street. I still could not catch my breath or stop crying and laughing. After having thought about Maharajji for the three years since I had first been with him, the unexpected shock of this meeting had left me ecstatic and confused.

The rickshaw led us through a number of small residential streets, and finally we stopped at a house, which Maharajji quickly entered. As we got down from the bus, the first thing I noticed was the smell of cooking. As we came up on the porch, the people greeted us as if we were expected. But how could this be? It turned out that early in the morning Maharajji had instructed the mothers of the house to prepare food for thirty-four people, who would be arriving in the late afternoon. How did he know? And wasn't it lucky that I had changed my mind and decided we should make the detour? Or perhaps there had been no "luck" involved at all. What this story reveals is that I, as a decision maker, am very suspect. And that just behind the stage may be an entirely different scenario from the one I think I am acting in.

This disquieting and at the same time refreshing reflection has a strong effect upon me. I stop taking myself so seriously. More often a small part of me is busy making choices, while by far the larger part is watching to see how it all comes out. Realizing there is meaning and purpose to events in life that are beyond the ken of my thinking mind—in other words, that I just can't understand what is happening—gives me equanimity. I'm less frightened about making the "wrong" choices.

The perspective about choice that this experience with Maharajji provided has led me to define my spiritual journey more as one of listening and tuning to what is than of choosing. The spiritual journey, as I now conceive of it, is a progression from truth to ever-deepening truth. I feel myself being drawn toward truth. I have taken guidance in this emphasis from Mahatma Gandhi, for whom "Truth is God." He saw his life as a series of experiments with truth and made every effort to align his choices with the deeper truths of the universe. This alignment with truth gives Gandhi's words an incredible moral force. So I listen at each choice point to hear the deepest possible truth from which to act, and I choose, realizing full well the paradox that I am both making the choice and not making the choice.

"Old as I am in age," Gandhi said, "I have no feeling that I have ceased to grow inwardly or that my growth will stop at the dissolution of the flesh. What I am concerned with is my readiness to obey the call of Truth, my God, from moment to moment, no matter how inconsistent it may appear. My commitment is to Truth, not to consistency."

I look back and see my own inconsistencies over time. I see how many things I have been wrong about in my life. I remember the arrogance with which I taught a course in human motivation at Harvard. How limited and even incorrect was the gospel according to behaviorism that I was propagating. I taught Freudian theory as if it were ultimate wisdom, while, in fact, it turned out to represent a rather impoverished view of the human condition. These and so many, many more.

How do I feel about all these errors? Embarrassed? A little! But that state of mind just flickers across the screen of consciousness. It is almost immediately replaced by a sense of humor at how poignant we human beings are. That, in turn, is replaced by a deep appreciation for the grace of having been able to move on, of not getting stuck in any particular take on reality, of seeing and being willing to admit my bad judgment. Truth isn't necessarily popular or easy to espouse, but it certainly keeps things lively.

A woman once came to Gandhi with her young son. "Mahatma-ji, tell my son to stop eating sugar. It's not good for him." Gandhi told her to return with her son in a week's time. When they returned, Gandhi said to the boy, "Stop eating sugar." The woman was perplexed and asked Gandhi why he couldn't have told the boy that a week earlier. Gandhi replied, "Because at that time *I* had not given up sugar."

What I feel is that the truth, as well as I can express what I can understand of it, is a gift I can give to another person. By offering them my truth as I know it, I am also offering them the message that the situation is safe. I am not consciously hiding anything. It's a little like a wolf baring its neck to another wolf. The other wolf then feels safe and stops fighting. We live in such a disturbing, paranoid world that a whiff of truth is like the most wonderful music. It may be difficult to hear, but it speaks directly to our hearts and invites them out to play.

Whether I speak the truth or withhold it depends, of

course, on the situation. Some people don't want the truth. I may be with a person who is obviously dying and simultaneously denying it. Unless the person asks me outright, "Am I going to die?" or words to that effect, I don't try to force her or him to face it. What is important for the potentially heart-networking communication is that I not knowingly lie and am willing to share my truth if I sense that it is appropriate.

Many times I've played the truth game with another person. We sit looking into each other's eyes and take turns saying, "If there is anything that you would rather not share with me because it is too difficult, embarrassing, inappropriate, trivial, whatever—share it." When I am asked that question, you can be assured that the most embarrassing thing imaginable, which I may never have thought about before, comes into my mind. Then, uncensored if possible, I answer the question. Then both of us sit quietly together contemplating the answer, until we have digested it. To digest it is to get by one's reactivity until one can see the response and all it implies as just another poignant part of the human condition.

With this method we either very quickly melt into the shared awareness that is true love or we meet a resistance in our collective psyche. We cannot tell what fear awakens the resistance in which of us, but here we stop. To do more would attempt violence, which would be fruitless. Stopping is not a failure. There was no necessary accomplishment. We did what we did and faced what we were ready to face. And that is this moment's truth. And there is sweetness in sharing just that.

• • •

I sit on the edge of the bed and hold Jean's hand. The oxygen tank that stands by the head of her bed is the jarring reminder in this otherwise soft and tasteful room that death is at hand. Jean's skin is blue-white transparent. Her hand, with its skin and veins and bone, now devoid of the flesh that gives body, is the hand of my dying mother, the hand of all dying mothers.

Jean says, "Ram Dass, I'm so bored. I wish it would be over." I have met Jean only once, briefly, several years before, but her request to see me and her deep Quaker roots and meditative practice encourage me to share my truth with her.

"You're bored because you're spending all your time dying. Any role, if you try to invest it with exclusive reality, is boring. Couldn't you die, say, ten minutes an hour?"

She laughs. I am remembering a seminar with Elisabeth Kübler-Ross, in which a nurse with metastasized cancer and young children showed us how our reactivity to her condition—with our pity, anger, shock, and so on—trapped her in the role of being a "dying person." She had said, "Everyone is so busy reacting to my situation, nobody is with me."

Jean squeezes my hand and tells me of a recurring vision of a frightening being circling a tree in which a small child is sitting. I encourage her to get to know the frightening being and see what, if anything, is really so frightening. She does her work silently; I can feel her body tensing and relaxing.

"Ram Dass, I feel everything is too much. The light, the sound. It's all overwhelming."

"Jean, you are opening to new energies. You are like a

one-quart container into which you are trying to pour two quarts of water. Perhaps you aren't a one-quart container after all. Let's try an experiment and expand together. Listen . . . do you hear the children playing outside? Instead of pushing against them as not-us, let's expand outward to include them inside ourselves. And the light coming in under the drawn shade, let the light be part of our bodies. Let's keep expanding to contain it all. Me and my voice—all within you, just as you are within me. But is there still a "you" and a "me"? As the boundaries soften, become permeable, and dissolve, feel how we merge . . . just one awareness."

We sit there for many minutes in the deepest peace, fully present in the moment, our hearts knowing the truth of love. Then Jean sits up and reaches out to embrace me. We hold each other and kiss. It is the kiss of recognition and celebration.

I gently lay Jean back on the bed. She closes her eyes now, all trying, all intention at rest. After a few minutes I get up and say, "Jean, you know what I know. It's only forms that change, not essence. Enjoy the changes. Goodbye."

Her gentle, attentive husband, who replaces me at her bedside, told me that she died a few hours later . . . peacefully.

There was a period of several weeks in 1972 when Maharajji would summon me many times a day. Each time I would hasten to him, sit down in front of him, and wait. Then he would either say, "Ram Dass, always tell the truth" or "Ram Dass, love everyone!" I'd usually answer something lame, such as, "I'll try," and then he would send me away. Day after day this went on, and I was getting more and more agitated because, the truth was, I didn't love everybody. Which should I do? Make believe I love everyone or tell the truth? I acknowledged that in the past I was more likely to make believe that I loved everybody than I was to tell the truth. So, for a change, why not tell the truth? For the next week I lived out the truth. And the truth was that I didn't really like any of the people around me, for one righteous reason or another.

At that time, as an experiment, I was not carrying money. So when I went on the bus, one of my friends would serve as my "bagman" and pay for me. But once I was mad at everybody, there went my bagman. When everybody else got on the bus to go the eight miles to the temple to be with Maharajji, I walked. It took hours to get there by a mountain path. When I finally arrived, everyone was eating lunch, and they obviously had had much time with Maharajji. This made me all the more angry. When one of the people, whom I particularly despised, offered me a plate of food, I threw the food in his face.

The next thing I heard was Maharajji calling, "Ram Dass!" I realized that he had seen my act, and I went to him feeling really miserable. When I was settled before him, he asked, "Something troubling you?" It was all I needed. I broke into sobs. Maharajji patted me on the head and pulled my beard, and he was crying too. He sent for milk and fed it to me. When I was finally able to speak, I blurted out, "I hate all those people," pointing at the Westerners across the yard, "and I hate myself, too."

"I thought I told you to love everyone."

"You told me to tell the truth. The truth is, I don't love everyone."

Then Maharajji drew close, nose to nose, looked very coolly at me, and said, "Love everyone and tell the truth."

At that moment I saw before me a coffin in which lay the person I thought I was. I heard Maharajji as if he was telling me exactly who I would be when I finished being who I thought I was. Whether he was goading me, giving me a boon, or creating a new reality, whatever he was doing, it worked. Now, nearly twenty years later, I hardly recognize myself, because my truth is coming to be that I love everyone. Well, not quite everyone. But I am working on it.

There was a time when my aggravation with the system focused on Caspar Weinberger, secretary of defense. I'm sure he was no worse than many others, but there was something about his cold arrogance and apparent lack of wisdom that infuriated me. So I got a picture of Caspar and placed it on my *puja* (prayer) table with all my spiritual heroes. Then, each morning when I lit my incense and honored the beings represented on the puja table, I'd feel waves of love and appreciation toward my guru, Buddha, Christ, Anandamayi Ma, Ramana Maharshi, and Hanuman. I'd wish them each good morning with such tenderness. Then I'd come to Caspar's picture, and I'd feel my heart constrict, and I'd hear the coldness in my voice as I said, "Good morning, Caspar." Each morning I'd see what a long way I still had to go.

But wasn't Caspar just another face of God? Couldn't I oppose his actions and still keep my heart open to him? Wouldn't it be harder for him to become free from the role he was obviously trapped in if I, with my mind, just kept reinforcing the traps by identifying him with his acts? I could see my guru rushing about in the wardrobe room at Central Casting, putting on one mask after another, shouting at me, "Bet you can't find me behind this one! Bet this one will really fool you!" Not the Caspar mask, Maharajji, no! Oh, *no*!

The Indian poet Kabir said, and Maharajji often repeated, "Do what you do to another person, but never put them out of your heart." It's a tall order. But what else is there to do? Sometimes there is really nothing to do. We can only work on ourselves to keep another person in our heart: to be there, open, waiting, loving, spacious, nonjudging, appreciating, . . . and listening.

So much of loving has to do with hearing another person and appreciating her or his predicament. In 1968 a woman came to visit me in the cabin on my father's estate to complain about her young daughter, who had forged her older sister's signature on a check. Her story was a lengthy one, concerning her own life as a single mother and seamstress after her husband had deserted her and the children. It was presented with much anguish and twisting of a handkerchief. I listened attentively while silently "doing my beads." When she finally finished I said, "I hear you!"

That statement didn't seem to satisfy her. I'm sure her recitation of this story, undoubtedly oft told in the past, usually elicited cluckings of pity, instructions, and such. So she said, "No, you don't understand," and began the recitation afresh, this time accompanied by tears.

When she had finished the second recitation, to which I had listened with attention, and during which she had let her eyes stay with mine for longer and longer times, I said again, "I hear you."

At my words this time, however, she smiled a rather roguish, little-girl smile and said, "You know, when I was a girl, I was kind of a hellion too." At that moment she relaxed, and there was subsequently a change in her perceptions and ways of dealing with her daughter.

Recently, in India, I visited Yeshe Dhonden, former personal physician to the Dalai Lama, and asked him for a diagnosis of my health. As he held my wrists, listening to my pulses, I understood a story I had told hundreds of times about him. He was invited to grand rounds at Yale Medical School and was diagnosing a patient. He stood holding her wrists, listening to her pulses, as Dr. Richard Selzer, who wrote the story, said, like a giant bird holding her hand in the most intimate way. After many minutes of this silent touch, he released her hand, having spoken not a word. As he went to leave the room, he turned back toward the bed and the woman, who was now holding her own wrist with her other hand, called out, "Thank you, Doctor." Dr. Selzer described how he personally felt envious watching this scene. "I was envious not of him, not of Yeshe Dhonden for his gift of beauty and holiness, but of her. I wanted to be held like that, touched so, *received*." I too felt heard and received.

In the late seventies, I experienced being heard and attended to in a manner that was extraordinarily subtle and profound. The experience was palpably healing. I had been invited by John and Toni Lilly to swim with Joe and Rosie, the dolphins with whom they worked. I was eager, because, in the circles in which I traveled, everyone wanted to swim with dolphins.

The day on which we had scheduled the swim at Marine World in Redwood City, south of San Francisco, was gray and cold. And as I watched my friend Peter in the water with the dolphins, who now seemed very large to me, I was having second thoughts. I was cold, and I couldn't quite remember why I had wanted to swim with the dolphins in the first place. But everyone stood at the edge of the tank watching, and it was too late to back down, so I climbed onto the platform in the tank and let myself into the chilly water. Both dolphins made flashing passes close by me. They were even bigger and more powerful than they looked from the tank's edge, and I was feeling very vulnerable in their territory.

Rosie stopped and hovered within arm's reach of me. I wanted to touch her, but that seemed a strange thing to do at that moment. My mental category system had her placed somewhere between shark and fish, neither of which would welcome my touch. I was desperately trying to remember what I was supposed to do. Everyone was watching. Finally, I reached out tentatively and ran a finger along her side. She didn't move at my touch, and it felt wonderful. So I touched her again with my whole hand. Her skin was as soft as anything I'd ever touched, and although she was now definitely aware that I was touching her, she still didn't move.

Suddenly I was infused with a feeling of her intimate, attentive, nonjudging presence. My own gross thoughts of panic and planning seemed like a prison, and I just let go—of fear, of intellectual analysis, of thought itself. My hand started to caress Rosie, and I laughed aloud. At that point Rosie flipped until she was vertical in front of me, her belly against mine. I hugged her and even kissed her. She pressed her body against mine.

All at once I began to get aroused. I panicked! Everyone was watching! Was it even legal, let alone normal, to be caressing a dolphin? But I felt so free I found I didn't really care. Soon afterward Rosie moved in under my arm, and after some trial and error I discovered how to hold tight to her, and we went swimming wildly around the tank. Each time after an ecstatic forty seconds or so I'd think, It's all well and good for you, Rosie, but I have to breathe. Just this thought, barely perceived by me, was enough to bring Rosie to the surface, where I could fill my lungs.

At one point we came up and people were taking pictures and I got to hamming it up—old Ram Dass and the dolphin—and I forgot to get a breath when she dove. But it wasn't more than a few seconds before she rose again to the surface, understanding in some wonderfully intimate way that I had a problem.

We swam like this for some time, until I began shaking with cold and turning blue. Then Rosie shook me off, got Joe, and the two of them with their noses forced me to the platform and out of the tank. Rosie had heard me so well because I felt her to be inside me. It felt the same as it had with Maharajji. There was nowhere to go and no need to hide. It was that unconditioned and unconditional love again.

Such love passes from Rosie and Maharajji to me, and from my heart it passes to others. I hold a boy dying of AIDS. I am gentle. My face is buried in his hair. Our hearts are open. Right here . . . right here, inside our hearts, we are not dying boy and kindly man, we are two beings, recognizing each other through and behind the drama. We share the awe of the moment, the peace that lies at the center of the whirlwind of fear and confusion. In that timeless moment, it is enough for both of us. We are healed. We are in the domain of love. We are free.

Now, I am freed by being in love with people. There is no possessiveness in it. It isn't really romantic. It's as though we are sharing one space, we have merged in love. It's the space that more and more I share with Maharajji, as the years go by. Even to be away from it in forgetfulness for a moment is very painful.

When I am searching for the ways to stay in love, I hear Maharajji saying, "Feed people, serve people, love everybody, tell the truth." So I serve more . . . and I find myself more in love. What is wonderful is that the love lies not outside as a reward, like a gold star for being a good helper, but within the act itself. For when you offer yourself in service, it opens your own heart so that you may once again taste the sweetness of your own heart's innate compassion.

Rabindranath Tagore, the great Indian poet, said, "I slept and dreamt that life was joy. I awoke and saw that life was duty [dharma]. I acted, and behold, duty was joy!"

And Gandhi said, "When you surrender completely to God, as the only Truth worth having, you find yourself in the service of all that exists. It becomes your joy and recreation. You never tire of serving others."

We are all part of a huge family. Within the family our acts of caring, insignificant as they may seem, are

nevertheless an integral part of a vast network of compassionate acts that are occurring throughout the universe
at each moment. Just as billions of tiny acts of ignorance,
greed, violence, and exploitation have created most of the
suffering and breakdown that now exist, so the billions of
tiny actions of compassion—which includes wisdom and
skillful means and joy—preserve and heal the situation.

While in Madras in South India, I was asked by one of
my guru's devotees to join him and his family in celebrating his birthday. We were to meet outside my hotel
entrance the next morning at seven thirty. It seemed a
strange time to celebrate a birthday. He arrived in his
car, which already contained his wife, son and daughter-
in-law, and daughter and son-in-law. As is the case with
all Indian transportation, there was room for one more.
We drove through the city in the early morning toward
the birthday celebration. I was mystified about what kind
it would be.

On the far side of Madras, we entered the gates of what
appeared to be a very poor ashram. In fact it turned out
to be the poorest ashram in the city. It was a home for the
destitute aged and the mentally disturbed. My host drove
the car into the middle of the courtyard. There were
several hundred inmates standing there, each holding a
tin plate. When the trunk of the car was opened, there
were huge covered pots of steaming rice and vegetables
and wonderful Indian sweets. Each of us was given a pail
and a ladle. We filled the pails again and again from the
pots, serving the contents to all the people now sitting
cross-legged on the ground in rows. When all had had
their fill, the sweets were distributed, and the ashram
served tea.

The pots empty and the utensils back in the trunk, we drove out of the ashram gates. In the car we were all silent, each alone with his or her own reflections and images gathered from such an intense experience. There were tears in all of our eyes. My host broke the silence with the words "Now, *that* was a birthday party."

The Path of Action

As I open to the love in my heart for my fellow beings—including the earth—and to my own interdependence and, indeed, identity with all beings, the yearning to become an instrument for the relief of all suffering grows stronger. Over time, the link between my spiritual growth and the possibility of becoming such an instrument has become clearer to me. As a result of my inner work, barriers have fallen away, allowing me access to sources of deeper compassion in myself. And out of this deeper compassion have come actions that are more effective in relieving suffering.

What exactly is my inner work? It involves a process of awakening through unlearning overhabituated and underexamined thought patterns. Some of these thought patterns are barely conscious, even unconscious. Others are so familiar in my thought terrain that I no longer even

notice them. Slowly, though, through my spiritual practices, I relinquish these habits of thought that have kept
me locked into my separateness, and I begin to remember
and reawaken to the way in which I am part of all
things—the unity of love that lies behind diversity. Now
I finally appreciate that the goal of these practices is not
to deny my uniqueness as a separate entity but rather to
balance it by simultaneously acknowledging the unity.

Over the years, I have drawn from a wide variety of
spiritual or consciousness practices that have helped me
to regain my balance. Because I delight in reason, I find
useful practices in almost all religious traditions that call
into play my intellectual faculties. But so too do I love
the power and play of my emotions, so I find myself
attracted to specific devotional practices that work with
the heart. Similarly I find practices that work with my
sensual, reflective, and energetic natures. I have, at one
time or another, been drawn to and grown from all of
these practices.

For those of us, however, who find ourselves drawn
toward the relief of suffering in others, there is a unique
practice: the path of action. This spiritual path uses as its
vehicle for transformation our actions themselves; that is,
we gain internal freedom through external action. Actions ranging from the most mundane to the most extraordinary can be used. While all actions are potentially
useful on the path of action, often the actions most readily
associated with the path are acts of service. There is an
elegance in the use of our acts of service for our spiritual
work. It lies in the fact that the very acts that we perform
to relieve the suffering of another being, be they through
offering a glass of water, holding a hand, building a road,

or protesting against injustice, can also serve as grist for the mill of our own spiritual growth, which, in turn, improves the effectiveness of our caring acts. It's like a self-sharpening appliance that improves with use.

Realizing that an enlightened being would be the most skillful in relieving suffering, I was for a time tempted to refrain from serving others until I had attained spiritual freedom. But whether that state would be reached in this life or many lives down the road was uncertain. Furthermore, I had to admit that it is really impossible to stop acting. As long as we are incarnates, we must act, and our actions will always affect others. Recognizing this, we can, as best as we are able, act for the benefit of all beings, knowing full well that our actions, not being those of a fully enlightened being, are a mixed blessing for others.

Because karma yoga, or the "path of action," is such a significant component of my spiritual practice, I wanted to understand it better—to clarify my own work as well as to help others gain clarity about theirs. As I have reviewed the literature, I have found that there is still a need to articulate this path in a way that makes it available to those of us with Western minds. Although the path of action represents different things to different people, there are common components that I have been able to identify. These are appropriateness, an awakening context, our relationship to the goal of the act, our relationship to the act itself, and the proficiency with which we perform the act. Beyond and intertwined with these are meditative and devotional components, which also play key roles. Let's examine all of these, and consider the way in which they unfold.

APPROPRIATENESS

On the path of action we need to act from our deepest intuitive appreciation of what is appropriate in the moment. To be able to do this, we must ask ourselves whether each act

- is in harmony with our values
- uses our particular skills, talents, and personality characteristics
- makes use of our opportunities
- acknowledges our liabilities as well as our assets
- takes into account our existing responsibilities
- is honoring the diverse roles we are called upon to fulfill in the moment

It isn't easy to take all these things into consideration for each action, or even the most important acts in our lives. Fortunately, however, we can call into play our intuitive mind, with its capacity to understand the gestalt, or total picture. We can intuit from moment to moment whether an act is fitting or appropriate for us. Of course, while any such choice may be right for the present moment, the intuitive listening cannot stop, because conditions keep changing, and what is appropriate one moment may not be so the next. We must be willing to correct our course of action again and again, never sacrificing truth for consistency.

In the West, the word that best describes the result of the process of intuitive listening for the course of our actions is *vocation,* which is defined as "a summons or strong inclination to a particular state or course of action." In a religious context, this means "a divine calling to the religious life."

In the East, these appropriate actions are called *dharma*. And in the *Bhagavad Gita*, the basic Hindu text on the path of action, we are enjoined to perform our own dharma. It is better to perform our own dharma imperfectly than to perform the dharma of another. At the time and place that the *Gita* was composed, there were precise external criteria that were used for determining vocation or dharma, that is, what was an appropriate action at a certain stage of life. Family lineage and age both played a part in this determination. In Western society, which so cherishes external freedom, we are not rigidly constrained by these external considerations. Thus, in the absence of such a simple road map, we must rely far more heavily upon our intuition to discover the appropriateness of our actions.

I find it necessary to listen freshly again and again to my inner voice. But to hear that "still small voice within" requires a quiet mind, not one weighed down with the baggage of distorting desires and unexamined habits of thought. To achieve this quietness requires meditation practice and some patience. The Chinese book of wisdom the *Tao Te Ching* asks,

> Do you have the patience to wait
>   till your mud settles and the water is clear?
> Can you remain unmoving
>   till the right action arises by itself?

For me, continuing meditative practice over twenty years has proved invaluable in the moment-to-moment quieting of my mind so that I could discern the appropriate action.

AN AWAKENING CONTEXT

The context in which an action occurs is critical in determining whether the act is indeed a part of the path of action. I may act simply to gratify a personal desire or I may perform the same act as a member of my family, my country, or a group sharing an ideological belief system. Acts performed for any of these reasons may be good or righteous, and as a result I may grow spiritually whether I realize it or not. But, for an act to be part of a "path," we must have the intention to grow or awaken. We perform the act because we believe liberation is possible and that this particular act may help us become liberated.

For example, there may be many reasons why I am sitting at the bedside of a dying person. I may be attached to that person, I may be a relative or a hospital volunteer, or an attendant or minister earning my living by sitting there. But whatever the reason I am sitting there, the path of action requires that I consider the act one that I will use for inner growth or awakening.

G. I. Gurdjieff, the Russian mystic and teacher, said that we need to recognize that we are in prison if we are to use what is available in the situation to escape. Obviously if we don't think that we are in prison, we won't make any attempt to escape. Similarly, if we think that material existence as we know it through our senses and our thoughts is all there is, then we will not be motivated to explore those aspects of ourselves that are not part of the material world. Once we start to realize that there is more to life than meets the eye, we can use all our actions to help us plumb the mystery of what else there might be. This is the path of action.

There are many ways to characterize what we are awakening from and what we are awakening to. For example, we may be awakening from an illusion into reality. We may be finding our "center" or a vantage point of spacious awareness. Or we may be escaping from a conditioned reality into an unconditioned state. We may be beginning to get a taste for the deeper truth that lies behind appearances. We may be reestablishing a balance between unity and diversity by working to reawaken our identity with the unity that lies within and beyond the diversity of all things. Any of these characterizations of the spiritual journey will suffice to provide an awakening context.

In addition to these ways of understanding the journey, there are devotional ways. The intention to remember and celebrate God is an act of devotion. We may consider God as our beloved and see each act as an offering or service or demonstration of our love. For me, the beloved appears in the form of my guru, Neem Karoli Baba. Thus I see my acts in relationship to him, as an offering of flowers, which I place at his feet.

Mother Teresa, the Nobel Prize–winning nun who has served the poor in the streets of Calcutta, speaks of her ministrations to the lepers she finds in the streets, befouled with vomit, excrement, flies, and filth, as "caring

for my beloved Christ in his more distressing disguises."
She is responding to the injunction in Matthew 25, where
Christ says, "For I was hungry and you gave me food, I
was thirsty and you gave me drink, I was a stranger and
you welcomed me, I was naked and you clothed me, I was
sick and you visited me, I was in prison and you came to
me. . . . Truly, I say to you, as you did it to one of the
least of these my brethren, you did it to me." And undoubtedly also to Isaiah 58:6–9:

> Is not this what I require of you as a fast: to loose the
> fetters of injustice, to untie the knots of the yoke, to snap
> every yoke and set free those who have been crushed? Is
> it not sharing your food with the hungry, taking the
> homeless poor into your house, clothing the naked when
> you meet them and never evading a duty to your kins-
> folk? Then shall your light break forth like the dawn and
> soon you will grow healthy like a wound newly healed;
> your own righteousness shall be your vanguard and the
> glory of the Lord your rearguard. Then, if you call, the
> Lord will answer; if you cry to him, he will say, "Here
> I am."

And also probably to Ecclesiastes 7: "Be not wanting in
comforting them that weep and walk with them that
mourn. Be not slow to visit the sick for by these things
thou shalt be confirmed in love."

I use all of these contexts to frame my actions. Sometimes I feel devotional and at other times I don't. I seem
to slip in and out of these contexts naturally and without
effort. But, for an act to serve as a vehicle for awakening,
at least one of these contexts must be present.

RELATIONSHIP TO THE GOAL

How do these awakening contexts for our actions fit with our immediate motivation for performing an act? For example, if I do something for someone, I'd like that person to be happy as a consequence. If I am giving a lecture, I'd like the audience to be enriched by what I say. If I am protesting against injustice, I'd like the protest to be heard and the injustice remedied.

Consider, for example, campaigning for an ecological issue. The immediate goal may be to gain media attention. That goal is instrumental in realizing a further objective of changing legislation, awakening the public conscience, or influencing the economic policies of the business community. In this situation, there are many factors beyond our control that determine whether our actions will realize their objective. A world figure may die just as a major article we have worked long and hard upon is about to appear in the newspaper, and our story may be dropped. We did what we could, but we were unable to control the rest of the news. Of course, it's a disappointment not to achieve our ends. However, we adjust our course, make corrections, listen afresh, modify those aspects of the system that are malfunctioning, and get on with it. After all, what else is there to do?

This capacity to work with failure as well as success in terms of immediate goals is enhanced immeasurably when we have, in addition, the overriding goal of awakening. Because both success and failure with regard to the immediate goal serve the spiritual practice, there is a balance in our perspective. That balance provides the conditions for equanimity in us, because we appreciate that while our act may not lead to the expected fruits in the short term, ultimately the act will have served to relieve suffering. If we are now able to remain calm, and not be burdened with agitation, anger, or frustration over the failure of our efforts, we are in the best position to hear what to do next.

Of course, being human—as most of us still are—when we fail in our efforts, we feel some degree of discouragement, frustration, depression, loss of confidence, flagging interest, anger, horror at our inability to relieve another person's suffering, betrayal, naïveté, stupidity, guilt, and a wide range of other reactions. By contrast, if we succeed, in addition to the happiness of realizing our objective and perhaps truly helping another being, we may feel inordinate pride, self-satisfaction, arrogance, a sense that we know it all, and a host of other interesting psychological hangers-on. I myself am certainly familiar with all of these.

I have learned that, in dealing with the effects of both success and failure, it is useful to have a vantage point or perspective sufficiently removed so that it can help me avoid becoming lost in any specific reaction. The vantage point allows me to see the larger processes at work, the ones made up of myriad successes and failures.

In the *Bhagavad Gita* we are enjoined to "be not attached to the fruits of the action." After all, if we are performing the action appropriate for us at this moment, doing it as skillfully as we are able, and attempting to use it as a means of awakening, then we have done what we can to realize the immediate fruits of the action. Being attached to realizing the goals will not make us any more effective. I have found that a strong identification with a desire for a specific goal can engender anxiety. The goal itself can assume fearful and sometimes debilitating proportions. I am amused when I remember that I did my doctoral dissertation on just this kind of achievement anxiety, typing it with hands swollen by anxiety-provoked dermatitis.

Our goals, of course, are direct reflections of our desires. The stronger our identity with any desire, the more we become attached to the goal. When our desires are strong, and we are identified with them, we often come to perceive the world in terms of objects to be manipulated in order to bring about our goals. This relationship to our environment is alienating, exploitative, and not good for our hearts. Realizing this, we can seek to free ourselves from identifying with our desires. We will continue to have desires, of course, but we learn to separate our awareness or identity from them. For me, such awareness is like the sky, and my desires are like clouds or planes, coming and going through the sky.

In order to break the identification with specific desires, I cultivate another desire—the desire to awaken through resting in spacious awareness—and use that desire as an overriding motive. As I am more established in that spacious awareness, the other motives lose some of their power because, from the viewpoint of awakening, whether I succeed or fail in any specific act does not matter. I come to see that appreciation by others, fame and shame, loss and gain, and even pleasure and pain are all teachings that help me with my inner growth. At a later stage still, I come to realize that I must forgo even my identification with the desire to awaken, for ultimately the identification with any desire keeps us separate from the truth. Here I face the paradox that I can only realize truth by not desiring it.

On the path of action, we are like a bookkeeper in a large company. The bookkeeper does the accounts, but whether there is a profit or loss is not her or his concern. We do what we do each day, we do it as impeccably as possible, and then we are at peace, realizing that the results are out of our hands.

People on the path of action may seem goal-oriented, but they also have a peacefulness that comes from non-attachment. The *Bhagavad Gita* says that as we progress on the path of action we come to "work as one who is ambitious, respect individual life as one who desires it, and are happy as those who live for happiness." But through it all we are, as the *Tao Te Ching* suggests, travelers who are enjoying the journey because we are not intent upon arriving.

That is all well and good, but when we are trying to relieve someone's suffering and our actions do not bring about that end, our hearts are often heavy. The risk of standing back is that we will not become fully engaged in each situation, that we will stand back in order to avoid this heaviness of heart, that we will not act "compassionately" (with passion). But it is possible, when we have developed a sense of balance, to engage in actions with passion while still perceiving from a more remote vantage point. Christ speaks of it as being "in the world, but not of it."

So we entertain the possibility that a part of us can be deeply involved in what we are doing while another part watches our moment-to-moment successes and failures with disinterest. The more remote part is motivated by a different set of purposes, no less admirable. It wants us to grow in wisdom and spiritual awareness. And from its vantage point it sees a way to use both our successes and our failures to this end. This greater aspiration also includes the relief of suffering, as, for example, in the case of the bodhisattva in Tibetan Buddhism, who seeks liberation for the benefit of all beings.

RELATIONSHIP TO THE ACT

"One does nothing and nothing is left undone." This mystical injunction points to one of the key components of the path of action: nonidentification with being the actor. I had always assumed that I had to identify with a role while performing in order to do it well. But each of us performs hundreds of acts each day—walking, blinking, driving, or knitting—to which we pay little, if any, conscious attention, yet we usually perform them quite well. It is now clear to me that very complex and creative acts often take place without our experiencing ourselves as actors. I think once again of the *Bhagavad Gita,* in which Krishna, who represents higher wisdom, reminds the seeker after freedom not to be caught up in thinking of himself as the doer. He says, "Only the fool whose mind is deluded by egoism considers himself to be the doer."

Many actors, musicians, artists, and teachers report entering a space during a performance or at work in which connection of the self to the act disappears. At precious moments, I have had experiences in which the act seems to be occurring by itself as a result of its connections with everything else. It sometimes happens when I am lecturing. Under these circumstances I have experienced myself as disappearing entirely or being a dispassionate observer from a distance. Certainly at those moments there is no actor.

The Japanese master Hakuin said, "Your coming and going is nowhere but where you are." This statement points to where you stand in the midst of action, even that arising from you. You stand in the quiet center, in the present moment, at peace.

PROFICIENCY

The path of action calls upon us to perform each action with discriminating wisdom and skillful means. That is, whatever the task, be it washing a dish or creating a masterpiece, we bring to the situation our full attention, our appreciation of the situation, and our skill in the performance of the action. A concentrated mind is of great importance in carrying out an act with proficiency. Similarly, a stance of mindfulness, in which we witness just what is, helps us determine not only the appropriateness of an action but the skillful means with which to carry it out. Once again we see the role that meditation plays in the path of action.

The effort to perform the act perfectly is further enhanced by devotion. In serving the beloved, how could we act in any other way than by giving our best? It is also enhanced by nonidentification with the actor and nonattachment to the fruits of the action. With the quietness of mind that these conditions bring us, we are able to hear the moment because we are fully in it. Under these circumstances, the moment takes on a rich immediacy that imbues it with a living spirit in which our acts truly approach perfection.

THE PROCESS

In pursuing the path of action, I have begun to see recognizable stages in the transformative process. At first I saw myself as a separate entity full of needs and desires. My identity with these desires left me very attached to the fruits of my actions and thus willing to manipulate things and people, as if they were objects, to realize my goals. Then, with just a little awakening, I saw that the desires were unending and even the gratification of them was leaving me in an unsatisfactory alienated state. I saw that I would always be dissatisfied as long as I was caught up in my desires, and that under these conditions my actions could not express the highest level of compassion.

As I understood my predicament more clearly, the desire for liberation started to supplant other desires. This was the beginning of the path of action. Through mindfulness training I began to cultivate the part of me that was not identified with the desires. Desires arose and passed by with little clinging on my part to them. During this period my aversions and attractions, born of desires that remained, became painfully apparent. At first I was hard on myself for being so caught in the desire mind. With time, however, compassion toward myself began to develop, and I was able simply to note the arising of these various feelings of attraction and aversion. I found myself less affected by the success and failure of my efforts in each task. The ability to witness my reactions to these results increased. A quality of equanimity began to arise. I also noticed that each time an action was carried out even partially selflessly, it strengthened an identity with some force greater than myself and helped to free me from thinking of myself as separate.

Now I notice two things developing simultaneously. The first is an impersonality in my actions, almost as if someone else were performing them. There is a sense of my being an instrument of some compassionate force or mind deeper or higher than my own separate mind. It is difficult to describe. Sri Aurobindo, a great Indian holy person, spelled out in precise detail just how our minds surrender into and are supplanted by the higher, more universal mind. One way of describing what I experience is that it is as though I am a node in a large network of compassion. The biblical expression "Not my will but thine" reflects this moment-to-moment experience.

The other emerging quality is an intensification of the love that permeates actions. The universe of forms has become increasingly imbued with a radiance, an awesome, often bittersweet beauty, that makes each of my actions in the world feel like an act of devotion. Because it is new to me, I am often surprised by the feeling of love for other people, animals, and the earth that arises, often when I least expect it.

This feeling of treasuring other beings and serving them as the beloved makes me want to perform my acts even more skillfully, making each act an offering of beauty. The act of love draws me closer to whoever or whatever is before me, and with this closeness comes an intensification of empathy with joys and sufferings. Out of this arises a desire to alleviate suffering in the best possible way. Whether I am at the checkout counter in the supermarket, sharing a moment with a person facing a terminal illness, protesting in a political action, or dealing with a policeman who has stopped me on the highway, it is all a dialogue with the beloved, our interaction being a vehicle through which we meet and are together. This love grows until, as mystic poets have suggested, it could "start to equal the love that a mother has for her baby, that a miser has for her or his money, that a person has for her or his lover."

Seeing the world as the many faces of the beloved, and experiencing myself as an instrument of some higher compassionate force or mind, feels at times as though the beloved is serving the beloved. Where am I in this process? In the beginning, I felt that I was doing it. Then I felt that I was observing it. And now I sometimes find myself absent and the compassionate action just occurring, rising out of the momentary conditions of the situation, having little to do with me at all. Reflecting upon these moments, I have a better understanding of the mystical adage "Out of emptiness arises compassion."

In this process, what has happened to the desire for liberation? At the beginning, the desire to awaken for the benefit of all beings was my overriding motive. This served to shift my perspective and guide my behavior. But as a great karma yogi, Swami Vivekananda, pointed out, "This desire too must be relinquished, for finally, to identify with any desire keeps me separate from God." At this point, as the Third Chinese Patriarch of Zen described it, "Striving ceases, and rest in true faith is possible."

Although I can recognize the advanced stages of the path from momentary experiences, in my humanness, I still get caught in a number of desire systems that I am just barely able to watch. The desire for power is an example. It is not so much a conscious desire to have power over other people as a fascination with the nature of power, with worldly empires and their leaders, that can still catch me. Then there is the issue of righteousness. There is still in me something of the little boy who desires to do "good," so that he can be seen by himself and by others as good. And also there is still the desire to achieve and to accomplish, a desire that seems independent of what is being achieved or accomplished. As a psychologist, I suspect that all of these desires stem from a sense of inadequacy.

These areas of attachment are still present and often seem precariously close to ruling my life and overriding the desire for liberation. I find that staying at the edge of this danger zone provides the hottest fire for the needed transmutation, and thus the edge is the best place for practicing the path of action. Like watching a sailboat out on the ocean waves, now you see it, now you don't. Often just as I appear to be losing the deeper spiritual truth of my existence, the feeling of being caught awakens me and I bounce back. As a result of coming through each of these crises, I find myself stronger in my faith, and ever closer to being a true yogi, the being who dwells at the end of the path.

THE RESULT

Just what is a true yogi like? Although I am still a long way from being one, I have been blessed to know one. For me, my guru, Neem Karoli Baba, is the frame of reference for what is possible. Such a being acts out of a fearless freedom, his compassion expressed in breathtakingly unpredictable ways, at one moment miraculous and at the next quite mundane. Even in the midst of the strong passions of the moment, there is a deep inner calm and peacefulness, an indifference to the polarities of fame and shame, loss and gain, pleasure and pain, and even life and death. Such a being works not from a sense of duty or for a transformation of being but because her or his compassionate heart finds expression spontaneously in action. Krishna, in the *Bhagavad Gita,* says, "I have no duty to perform, nor is there anything in the three worlds unattained which is to be attained; still I am engaged in action." And, finally, in each action of a true karma yogi, there is love—unconditional love—expressed in the myriad ways that only a true lover can know.

Once we begin to understand the path of action, we still have many practical steps to take in finding our way into appropriate service. We have to begin somewhere. And often the beginnings are confusing or difficult. This section is a guide into the world of service, a little help on the path, some suggestions to ease the entry, a handbook for compassion in action.

FIRST STEPS

Mirabai Bush

Act from the Heart

*Let the beauty we love be what we do. There are a
hundred ways to kneel and kiss the ground.*

JALALUDDIN RUMI

In Springfield, Massachusetts, a group of people of
color—African-Americans, Latinos, Native Americans,
Cambodians, and Vietnamese—are watching their friends
and their friends' babies, whole families, die of AIDS.
More every day. They are sad and angry and frustrated.
But being people of color, some of them recent immi-
grants, they are less identified with mainstream thinking;
they know that there are other ways to see things. They
understand that the government-sponsored response to
AIDS in their community not only is not working but
does not come from a deep enough understanding of
healing the whole. They know that their community is
not healthy in many ways. Poverty, bad nutrition, inadequate health care, bad schools, lack of community gathering places, police brutality, and the simple exhaustion
that comes form trying to keep a family together in these

conditions have created an environment that is all too vulnerable to negative influences, whether it be AIDS or the Medellín cartel. The healing must be deep and wide. Recently, they planned a week of multicultural education and discussion that began with a Unity Day based on the Native American medicine wheel to begin to heal the whole community, of which AIDS is a part.

This is what compassion in action is about. Once we are called by the suffering around us—AIDS babies who won't stop crying, Native Americans losing their land, or the polluted stream in the woods near our home—the path of action encourages us to respond from deepest, most conscious, best informed, and most intuitive place we know. We bring everything we have to the situation, and we act—bravely—from the place in ourselves that we trust. We listen and question and look for ways that not only relieve the immediate suffering but also go to the root of the problem. We get in touch with who we are inside, and we remember that everyone else is very much like us, longing for basic human needs, for a peaceful and nourishing life, and for love. We remember that we all share that great gift, the human heart, and we try to keep it open and act from it.

When the people of Springfield brought the medicine wheel to the center of their program, they threw out the conventional public health models of how to run a conference and went straight to what they knew, to what their hearts told them would bring healing. For many of us wanting to change things, it feels too risky to listen to our hearts. We lean toward the conventional, the sensible, and the efficient, and we miss the opportunity to contribute what is most important about us—our own understanding of what is true and unifying. Of course, we need to be practical also, but only to serve what starts in the heart. This is the source of radical and enduring change. We need to listen for what we know to be true, and do what we love to do.

For example, soon after losing the election to Ronald Reagan, Jimmy and Rosalynn Carter went to work with Habitat for Humanity in Uganda and then on the Lower East Side of Manhattan. The former president of the United States and his wife, whom we might expect to be extremely "serious" about their next career decision, had volunteered to build small, inexpensive houses for the poor with an organization that believes that "every person should have a simple, decent house in which to live." They worked side by side with the future homeowners —and they loved it. "Rosalynn was never more beautiful," said Jimmy, "than when her face was covered with black smut from scraping ceiling joists, and streaked with sweat from carrying sheets of plywood from the street level up to the floor where we were working, cutting subflooring with a power saw, and nailing it down with just a few hard hammer blows." They had found something they loved and believed in, and they were doing it well. "Of all the activities we have undertaken since leaving the White House," said Jimmy more recently, "building houses with Habitat is certainly one of the most inspiring. The tiredness is all worthwhile, and sometimes the spirit soars." Many years later, the Carters are still giving a week a year to Habitat.

Art Serota is another example of someone listening for change from the heart. Art was a senior partner in a civil rights law firm with a practice in Springfield. After seventeen years and 5,000 cases representing young black and Latino men, he wanted to see what could be done earlier in their lives, before they reached the point where "they saw themselves as dumb and their lives as going nowhere." Moved "to be a personal witness to Africans not affected by North American slavery," he traveled six times to Zimbabwe, where he lived for three years, working in villages and cooperatives on agricultural, health, and school projects, where he discovered "environments in which it is safe to share goodness." Inspired by this discovery, he left the insulation of wearing a suit and the security of drawing a salary to start The Learning Tree, a community-based alternative learning center. The Learning Tree is a partly residential program for one of the least-served groups in the country: young black and Latino men who have dropped out of school.

At no cost to participants, The Learning Tree helps them get their high school equivalency diplomas and apply to college; it also focuses on vocational skills, creative expression, community service, self-esteem, and self-reliance. It is a place where it is safe to share goodness. Robert Castillo, a portrait painter who was sleeping in his car before coming to The Learning Tree, recently presented a portrait of her father to Malcolm X's daughter. His painting of Nelson Mandela was shown at a large gathering celebrating Mandela's release from prison. Others are now studying in local colleges, are using computers, have become writers, and have generally developed a sense of pride and possibility that will make needing a lawyer like Art much less likely. Ninety percent of the participants who start the program finish. The Learning Tree is by all measures a success, but it would not have existed if Art had been satisfied with his law practice and not explored what he really wanted to do.

We may need to think about service in a completely new way if we are to find an opportunity to do something we love. Our first thought may be to use our most expert skill, the thing we do best in our daily work, such as repairing cars, massaging aching bodies, practicing civil rights law, or negotiating international peace. But sometimes we need to look at our other talents and skills. We often think of these as hobbies—as the Carters probably did, having put in a tongue-and-groove floor in their attic in Plains—but these activities may be just what we need to perform truly effective service. Maybe we can heal the world through arranging flowers, writing poetry, or baking bread in a shelter. Why not? The "serious" methods that have been tried—from the war on poverty to the war in the Gulf—haven't ended the pain; often they seem to have created more. We need to free our minds if we are to find new paths through the dark forest of suffering. We need experimentation and playfulness in the face of difficulty, no matter how paradoxical that may seem. As Tibetan Buddhist teacher Tarthang Tulku says, "We already know how to enjoy ourselves. When we are enjoying ourselves, we are productive and creative. It's just a matter of bringing that enjoyment into everything we do."

Finding the time and space to do what we love can be difficult; we all already have full lives. So sometimes we have to change our present situation dramatically to make space, as Art did when he gave up his law practice, and sometimes we fit it into our existing life, especially when that life includes children or others who depend on us. A woman who is a mother, wife, homeowner, and therapist sees on television a South African policeman bring his club down hard on a black man's head; the man falls to the ground and people run over him in panic. She becomes haunted by the image and wonders what she can possibly do about human rights in South Africa. She wants to help, but she may not feel able to add more responsibility to her life. Once she thinks of something she'd like to do, she also has to make sure that it is not going to add so much stress to her life that she gives it up. She may make a better contribution addressing fly-ers or serving food at a fund-raiser, if she enjoys that, than devising a boycott strategy or traveling to Johan-nesburg, even if those options are in some ways appeal-ing. It's important to know what each of us loves and yet what each of us can do so that we can find service that is both appropriate and deep enough to be satis-fying and renewing.

This exercise may help you to find a means of service that will come from what you do well and love. Sit quietly. Either say out loud or write down the words "The way I'd really love to help is . . ." Keep it going.

One friend, who had been haunted by thoughts of people living in welfare hotels and on the streets, wrote, "The way I'd really love to help is to work with homeless mothers, because I know if I were homeless I would be scared and tired. But I don't know how I could be help-ful. What I'd really love to do is use my camera to take pictures, but what good would it do? What I'd really love to do is be together as people, not relating to houses but to each other. What I'd really love to do is have fun together because I know that when you are stressed it's

hard to have fun, but that doesn't sound right somehow. . . ." These rambling thoughts became a small
project, in which, after talking to homeless mothers
about what they would want, she taught them to pho-
tograph their children. The photographs became a gallery
show, which raised public awareness about the issue. To
go with the photographs of the children, she created
portraits of the mothers. The show was eloquent; people
saw the beauty, the humanity, the joy, and the sadness of
these families without homes. The young women not
only gained treasured photographs of their children but
developed the sense of mastery that comes from learning
a new skill. And our friend was able to do what she really
wanted to do.

Richard Sandler, by contrast, is an accomplished New
York photographer who is, among other things, a sta-
dium photographer for the New York Mets magazine.
Richard is also a journalistic photographer who shoots in
the street. One of his concerns is the number of homeless
people and the number of people walking by them without paying attention. His extraordinary images of these
two worlds coexisting inches apart without contact have
been shown in a number of galleries. While doing this
work, Richard also began to want to do something more
and something different, and he began to play the saxophone in a place that needed the healing and had interesting acoustics: the subway, where, as he says, "people
walk around in a bubble of territorial exclusion" that is
rarely penetrated. As he acted on this idea, two things
happened: the music at times entered the bubbles, surprising and waking people up with its beauty, and the
money that was dropped into his saxophone case he

dropped into the hands of the homeless who were also hanging around listening. The best response, he said, came from people who weren't asking for it but who clearly needed it. "The smiles on their faces were something to believe," he said. "What is this? Who am I? Is this really happening? Is this New York? It was fabulous." He knew this wasn't changing city policy on low-cost housing or real estate development, but it was what felt right for him at the time. And who doesn't understand what healing music can bring into the world?

We need to care more about one another and to ease one another's pain, or a great blanket of suffering is going to drift down and cover us in sadness. So start your list. "The way I'd really love to help is . . ." Joseph Campbell said that we are all trying to find what it is that we love to do "so that our life experiences on the purely physical plane will have resonances within our innermost being and reality, so that we feel the rapture of being alive." It's time to get started: to act from the heart, to do what we love with compassion, to walk together down one of those paths that leads home.

Listen

The music of life is in danger of being lost in the music of the voice.

MOHANDAS GANDHI

Pain and suffering may often seem to be calling us to jump in and fix things, but perhaps they are asking us first to be still enough to hear what can really help, what can truly get to the cause of this suffering, what will not only eliminate it now but prevent it from returning. So, before we act, we need to listen. When we do become quiet enough and "listen up," as we now say in the cities, the way opens, and we see the possibilities for action.

We give very little attention to learning to listen, learning to really hear another person or situation. Yet think back to the moments with other people when our hearts were engaged and we felt fed by being together. In those moments, weren't we hearing one another? In times like those, when we have listened to and heard one another, we have felt life arising from a shared perspective.

Each situation, each moment of life, is new. We and

this other person or group of people have never been here before. Oh, we've been in moments like it, but the present moment is new even if we have performed the same action with the same person hundreds of times before. Of course, it's easy to think, "Well, it's just like the last time, so I'll do what I did last time," and then not have to listen to the new moment. But if we do that, our lives become boring replications of what we have always done before, and we miss the possibilities of surprise, of new and more creative solutions, of mystery.

For our often humdrum lives to retain the taste of living truth, we have to listen freshly—again and again. A human interaction includes both the uniqueness of each being and the unity of the two, which transcends the separateness. For our minds to take such a subtle process and trivialize it to "just this again" or "nothing but that" is to reduce us to automatons, to objects for one another. And for action to be compassionate, we need to eliminate the idea of object, we need to be here together doing exactly what needs to be done to relieve pain and suffering in the simplest way we can. We need to listen.

Francis Giambrone, who has spent many years working with people with AIDS, tells how he began to learn to listen:

"I remember my first case. It wasn't AIDS, it was cancer. It was my first death case at the hospice. I would come in and say, 'Angelo, how are you?' and he would put on the television. Refused to talk to me. I would end up in his kitchen with his wife, and what was interesting was that I would think, Oh my God, here's my childhood. Dad is in the living room, won't communicate with me, and Mom and I are in the kitchen laughing and talking.

It was my parents Frank and Katherine and me, and it was Angelo and his wife and me. . . . And I thought, I'm going to do it differently this time.

"One day we were watching television and I lifted his foot and said, 'Angelo, look at your nails. They need to be cut.' And he looked at them and he said, 'Yeah.' I said, 'Do you want me to cut them?' And he said, 'All right.' And that, believe it or not, was the breakthrough. I sat there cutting his toenails and his fingernails, and slowly I asked him questions and I got him to talk.

"I had such strong ideas about what helping means. And what does it mean? It means *listening* and then do-ing. . . . I had been thinking, Angelo, this is how you are going to die. These are the books you are going to read. But a lot of dying people are not concerned about how they are going to die. They want to stay alive! This experience had an impact on all my work—even my non-dying work. I discovered that I'm not there to impose my reality on other people . . . I'm there to be a listener."

When we begin to act by listening, the rest follows naturally. It's not so easy, of course—it requires us to give up preconceived ideas, judgments, and desires in order to allow space to hear what is being said. True listening requires a deep respect and a genuine curiosity about situations as well as a willingness just to be there, to cut toenails and share stories. Listening opens the space, allows us to hear what needs to be done in that moment. It also allows us to hear when it is better *not* to act, which is sometimes a hard message to receive.

The music of our lives often gets lost in the music of our voices. We think that we already know what there is to hear. Sometimes we are simply moving a little too fast.

Recently the phone in a friend's kitchen rang; it was the organizer of a local project that was bringing Guatemalan village leaders to town for a three-week conference. "Yes," she said, before he had a chance to ask. "That's great. I have a house you could use for a gathering." "Thank you, that's very nice," he replied in his Puerto Rican accent that sounded like salsa music, "but what we really need is someone to drive them around." Ah, it's small, you may think, but there it is again—acting without listening. Isn't it at heart the same impulse that leads the World Bank to build a dam for villages that don't want the electric power it provides or the U.S. Agency for International Development to decide that a village needs a road to the market without asking the people if they have anything to sell there?

After working with the Sarvodaya village development movement in Sri Lanka—a people's movement based on the integration of spiritual and cultural values, community organization, and self-reliance—Joanna Macy described how its members learned that "what we really need to do is to go to the people, generate communication, and be unafraid to listen": "It was with the villagers first and foremost that Sarvodaya's founder Ariyaratna and his colleagues sought to communicate; and since true communication is a two-way street, that meant listening too. To listen with attention and respect is a skill that the Movement stressed, emphasizing that it is the villagers themselves who are, in the last analysis, the 'experts' on what they need and what they can do. Instead of coming in with preformulated blueprints for action, organizers instigate 'family gatherings' where the local community itself assesses its needs and determines its priorities by consensus. These provide, sometimes for the first time, the occasion where a broad cross section of villagers can listen to each other, too. Out of this interaction have grown the fresh and deceptively simple formulations through which Sarvodaya conveys its philosophy of development."

When playwright August Wilson (*Fences, Ma Rainey's Black Bottom*) was asked how he was able to express the reality of African-Americans so effectively (including those African-Americans who are very different from him), he said, "You have to listen. In the larger society, we are not listening to our kids, black *or* white. You may have to struggle to understand it because it's different from the world you know. For instance, if I go listen to rap, what these kids are doing these days is different from what I did as a teenager, and the way they're working out their social conduct is different from the way we did. So I simply say, 'Okay, I'll buy in on your terms, let me see what's going on with you.' "

There are now many people and organizations teaching techniques for clearer listening and appreciating the role of listening in the process of change. One such group is Rural Southern Voice for Peace, which has developed The Listening Project, a process by which members of grassroots groups go door to door or to familiar gathering places as they are beginning a project. They ask "open-ended questions in a non-judgmental but challenging way that encourages people to share their deepest thoughts" about the area of the group's concern. They report that "remarkable things happen as this process unfolds: Activists empathize with former 'opponents,' replacing negative stereotypes with understanding and concern; barriers are overcome as both sides experience common ground and see each other as human beings with deeply held hopes and fears. People being surveyed feel affirmed, sensing that what the listeners really want is to know their opinions; some start to change their opinions as they explore, often for the first time, their deeper feelings about social problems."

Listening to others clearly opens the way to understanding the helping situation. But listening to others requires quieting some of the voices that already exist within us. When this happens, there is space not only for the voices of others but for our own truest voice, what the Quakers call the still small voice within. This voice always tells us the truth. And, as Alice Walker has said, "The inner voice can be very scary sometimes. You listen, and then you go 'Do whut?' I don't wanna do that! But you still have to pay attention to it."

We need to take time to quiet down and listen to ourselves with attention—not only in the midst of action but when we are alone, walking in the woods, making tea, praying in an empty church, fishing in a stream, or sitting in meditation. A simple breath meditation can be helpful, because it returns us to a basic connection with the world. As we breathe in and out, and bring our awareness gently to our breath, we are experiencing the world coming into us and ourselves going back out into the world. We are reminded, in a simple physical way, that we are not separate from the world but continually interacting with it in the very makeup of our being.

Tiny Stacy, entertainment coordinator of the Blue Plate, a club in western Massachusetts, spends a big part of his life in service to others. He has organized many benefits, including one with Arlo Guthrie for Tibetan relief, and he has served as the Dalai Lama's chauffeur. It is meditation that has helped him learn to listen and to serve better. He describes it this way: "Your attention is focused, wholehearted. Meditation helps you bring awareness and caring into each action and each moment. It gives you a chance to deepen your awareness, to listen more fully. It led me to direct my life more toward service and less toward concern for myself."

We need to listen fully. It's the basis of all compassionate action. We need to listen not only to the voice of the person who is hurting but to her bare feet, the baby wrapped in her shawl, and the stars in the cold night. Such full listening helps us hear who is calling and what we can do in response. When we listen for the truth of a moment, we know better what to do and what not to do, when to act and when not to act. We hear that we are all here together, and we are all we've got. In Gandhi's terms, we are letting the music of our voices make way for the music of life.

Start Small

Small service is true service. . . .
The daisy, by the shadow that it casts,
Protects the lingering dewdrop from the sun.

WILLIAM WORDSWORTH

In recent years in North America it has been hard to escape painful social realities such as hunger, homelessness, illiteracy, and drug abuse. If all we read is the daily newspaper, we still learn more than we have ever before known about the complex and long-lasting causes of poverty and prejudice. It has become easy to feel overwhelmed by the enormity of the suffering and apathetic about the possibility of change. Derek Bok, as president of Harvard, wrote that "there is disturbing evidence to suggest that most forms of responsibility toward others have eroded in recent decades." And Charles M. Vest, president of Massachusetts Institute of Technology, said recently, "As I look around the nation, I do fear that we are throwing up our hands in the face of very difficult social and educational issues."

It can certainly look that grim. And as long as we see

suffering as an "issue" or a monolithic social problem, such as homelessness, hunger, or AIDS, we will find it difficult to act. The enormity of the suffering leaves us feeling dwarfed and powerless. And even a single person's pain may seem too big if we think of taking it on by ourselves.

Yet each of us can do something. Walking three miles to work won't heal the whole ozone layer, but it is something one person can do. And although we each can't do everything, together we can make a difference. Each of these bignesses is made up of many small parts. Individual people, sometimes working in groups. Individual moments. It is like the AIDS quilt, stitched together by the NAMES Project. Each patch is small, personal, and handmade. Each one reflects the person who made it and his or her friend, lover, or child who died of AIDS. Each patch is different: sweet, sophisticated, loving, stylish, outrageous. Together they make an immense blanket of love, care, sadness, and beauty. Like the Vietnam Veterans Memorial in Washington, D.C., which lists the names of all the Americans who died in that confusing war, it is difficult to see the quilt without feeling simultaneously the poignancy of each individual patch and the power of the entire statement.

Each small act is part of a great fabric. The AIDS quilt doesn't replace the need for government responsibility—it points to it. And it is interesting that the big problems are exactly the ones that may find their solutions in small, creative, offbeat, unlikely ideas.

New to Chicago, Bill McBride had just heard that his college roommate had AIDS. One night, in a neighborhood bar, he was handed a pamphlet describing a residence for people with AIDS. "We need help," the person who handed him the pamphlet said. "Will you help?" Surprised at himself, Bill agreed immediately.

With a friend for moral support, Bill arrived at Chicago House, a large home in the uptown section of the city. The director asked him what he could do. "Well," Bill said, "I am an editor and a teacher, so I guess I could read to people." "They don't want that," the director answered, but Bill persevered. "Well, I can cook—I grew up in the South—my mother taught me." "That might be good," the director said, "but don't come with any expectations. Maybe no one will eat the food." Apprehensive but willing to try, Bill returned a few nights later by subway with one of his favorite dishes. To his delight, it was a hit; it led to him being called Casserole Queen. And it came from a simple beginning, following the basic guidelines: be brave, start small, use what you've got, do something you enjoy, don't overcommit.

Later, as Bill began to appreciate the many problems associated with helping people with AIDS and to realize the need in the AIDS community for greater financial support, he wanted to do more. Working as an editor during the day and cooking at night, Bill, with the help of his friend Jim LiSacchi, thought of creating and marketing a cookbook that would benefit people with AIDS. Calling on help from some of Chicago's greatest chefs, they created *Specialties of the House: Great Recipes from Great Chicago Restaurants*. The dedication page reads: "To lend a helping hand in a time of need is to strengthen the spirit and compassion of all humanity." The book sold well, raised money for Chicago House, and became a model for similar projects in other cities.

There are opportunities everywhere. They may present themselves even when we stop at a neighborhood bar. A hospice worker adjusts a patient's pillow, a cabdriver at the end of her shift drives a pregnant woman to the hospital, a shelter "family" stands in a circle of silence before their meal, a development worker in Mexico keeps extra blankets in her apartment for visiting refugees. The small things carry a message of caring. They say that each one of us matters.

Amnesty International recruits volunteers to write letters to prisoners of conscience. It seems like a small thing to do. A Moroccan prisoner wrote back: "For us the letter is the outside, the forbidden! It increases the hope to see, some day in the future, unknown strands, the world of our imperfect dreams, the world of the living."

High school senior Asha Nadkarni volunteered to visit mentally retarded adults in a state school on their birthdays. She would take each patient a cupcake and a balloon. She reported, "Meeting these people was discovering a purity found in most children and envied by most adults. . . . Perhaps the touch of someone young brightened their day. Maybe they went to bed that night a little happier than the night before. It was a little thing I did; it's hard to save the world with a cupcake. But who couldn't use a birthday party?"

Small is, in fact, beautiful. Human-scale undertakings based on common sense are the most likely to succeed. As E. F. Schumacher said, "Small scale operations . . . are always less likely to be harmful than large scale ones.

There is wisdom in smallness even if only on account of the smallness and patchiness of human knowledge."

When Joanne Eccher and friends started the Hunger Hotline in Boston, their ambitious goals were to "get different legislation passed and do advocacy work with food pantries and soup kitchens and do litigation work to raise welfare benefits and get food stamps expanded." But when they met with the people in the community, they found that "the first thing they wanted was rats and roaches out of their pantries. And the next thing they wanted was better food at their meals. And then vans and transportation. And I remember thinking, Vans and transportation. We're just contributing to the charitable aspect. But after some time we realized that people's basic human needs had to be met and trust had to be established before they could begin to ask why they were in such a situation. We had to start with the small things before we could deal with the bigger issues."

When a project starts with a minimal investment and just a few people, there is little to lose; the project can take more risks, play closer to the edge, and reveal new ways of dealing with intractable problems. Such solutions can then be a model for others. Or the "multiplier effect" may occur, in which those people who learn in a small project teach others how to do something in their communities, and those people then teach more people.

During their Harvard Law School summers, Alan Khazei and Michael Brown had both worked in Washington for lawmakers trying to create a federally financed national youth service corps, a kind of domestic Peace

Corps. Their dream was of teenagers across the country giving a year of their lives to providing new life to America's cities while learning about teamwork, caring for others, the richness of social diversity, and the great feeling that comes from making a difference after you've worked hard. As the proposals lingered in congressional committees, they began to realize that there might be too many obstacles to starting with a government-sponsored, national plan, especially with a Republican administration governing a skeptical population. But they were still close enough to their own adolescence to remember its incredible energy looking for expression.

They returned to Boston and, after an experimental summer program, recruited fifty young people, seventeen to twenty-two years old. It was a racially, ethnically, economically, and socially diverse group—rich, poor, black, white, Latino, Asian, suburban preppy, inner-city gang—to "walk with, and help out, Boston's most vulnerable residents: the poor, the homeless, and the mentally and physically disabled." With money from foundations and corporations, City Year gives each of its members a stipend of $100 a week and a $5,000 college scholarship at the end of a year of service. The corps has started and now manages an after-school program for children at a low-income housing development. It has salvaged and distributed 130 tons of surplus food, painted a shelter for the homeless, and repaired and cleaned the homes of senior citizens in East Boston. In a ghetto storefront, the City Year team has tutored scores of Latino youths in reading and math and served as role models for them. It has carried out a census of the homeless, worked in nursing homes, and cleaned up a tot lot. Equally satisfying to Mike Brown, however, are the changes in the corps members themselves, whom he sees as developing the qualities of "involved citizenry," which he feels needs to be restored in our democracy if it is going to survive.

When we act, we can see our feelings of powerlessness dissolve. Movements such as the antiwar movement, the civil rights movement, and the labor movement began with individual acts by caring human beings such as Rosa Parks, who simply sat in the front of the bus, and Ron Kovic, who spoke out for veterans by speaking out for himself. At their most effective these movements were still simply the total of all those individual people acting to bring the changes they believed in. And, as some folks say, if Rosa Parks hadn't sat down, Martin Luther King, Jr., would never have stood up.

When we start small, we are more likely to remember that not only is it okay to be ourselves but in fact that is the most important thing. We can't be Martin Luther King, Jr., or Rosa Parks. We can be inspired by them, but even if we try we can't be them. We have to be ourselves. As ancient wisdom tells us, "Do not seek to follow in the footsteps of the men (or women) of old; seek what they sought." We have to look and see what *we* can do.

Tutoring can be a help. Childcare can be a help. Casseroles can be a help. There were many happy meals at Chicago House, during which people dying of AIDS told one another their stories and laughed about some of the absurdities of life. Maybe your style is brandied chicken with green peppercorns or hot apple cake with caramel-pecan sauce. Give it a try. Start small, and give yourself a chance to find out. Begin alone, or begin with others, but keep it simple. And remember the words of Margaret Mead, who said, "Never doubt that a small group of thoughtful, committed citizens can change the world; indeed it's the only thing that ever has."

Start Right Where You Are

. . . everything here
apparently needs us, this fleeting world,
which in some strange way
keeps calling to us. Us, the most
fleeting of all.

RAINER MARIA RILKE

Everything in our lives has brought us to exactly where we are. When we don't already know what is calling us to act, all we need to do is look and listen right where we are—it will probably be near. Maybe not geographically near, because our neighborhoods are not only physical, but it will be near.

When asked where she thought people should start looking, peace activist Fran Peavey said, "There are opportunities for service all the time. One time, driving a cab, I picked up a woman in her nightgown. She had been walking in her sleep and she was lost. I helped her find her way home. . . . Wherever you are, whatever you're doing, you can serve there. It doesn't have to be a big idea. It can be right where you are."

Frances Crowe, the "mother" of the peace movement in western Massachusetts, runs the local American

Friends Service Committee from the basement of her home in Northampton. For her, service began at the kitchen table, at home with her children. A young mother in the early fifties, when nuclear testing above ground was still considered safe by the government, she was married to a doctor who was beginning to realize the dangers of adding poisons such as strontium 90 to the atmosphere. The toxins were carried most readily through cows' milk, just as they were after the Chernobyl explosion. Her protective maternal energies awakened, Frances began buying milk that had been powdered before the tests. When she felt she had enough for her family, she began to buy more for her friends. In a moment of awakening, she realized that her care reached beyond her children and the children of her friends and that hoarding milk for an ever-increasing circle was not the answer to the problem. So she sat down, wrote notes to everyone she knew inviting them to a tea at her home to discuss the situation, and from that small gathering the nuclear freeze movement in that part of the country began, as did a group that is now resisting research and development of anthrax and other potential chemical and biological weapons.

As you read this, there is something that needs to be done. Suffering can be reduced and help can be offered. Just look around.

You are walking down the street in your neighborhood in Berkeley, thinking about world hunger, when you see a man in old clothes pull bread crusts and an ice cream cup from the trash and sit down on the curb to eat what is left. You know you have to do something. When Carolyn North found herself in this very situation, she says that she "fell apart." It was a turning point for her, happening right in her own neighborhood, right where she was. "It was emotionally clear to me that I would not be comfortable eating another meal unless I did something about hunger locally." She called food kitchens and began to attract donors, and soon she had started Daily Bread, which became a well-developed organization of volunteers who pick up food at bakeries and restaurants in Berkeley and Oakland and deliver it to food kitchens and shelters.

One Sunday morning, Darrill Bazzy woke up early in his apartment in the North End of Boston, where he slept on a mat on the floor, to the noises of an unhappy family below him, fighting among themselves. He says, "Now I look back and wonder what I could have done to help that family, but then I just wanted a calm and peaceful place to go. I was still frightened by the neighborhood. I went to a church that's on the historic trail, a beautiful, white colonial church with a pipe organ, so I could listen to the music. At the end of the service, they announced, 'We have room for two more people to go to Saint Lucia island and build houses for widows. You don't have to belong to the church to come along.' I thought, Okay. Sure. And I went. And I learned some amazing lessons. And it was someone I worked with there who called me two years later and asked if I wanted to go to Honduras."

In every community, there are calls for help. If you are interested in working to relieve hunger, for example, any small effort will be appreciated by the people who work in the various shelters and soup kitchens in your area. You can work as an accountant or proposal writer to raise funds. You can fix broken trucks or use your own vehicle to collect food. You can glean usable products from donated damaged goods, working alongside others in a warehouse. You can package bread and muffins. You can answer phones. You can type letters or pack bags of groceries. You can play the piano in a soup kitchen, cook a meal, or put together menus from the ingredients at hand. You can make sure your company, your neighborhood market, or your local bakeries and restaurants recycle their leftover food, and, if they don't, you can salvage it yourself. These are just a few of the possibilities, and these just relate to hunger. Look around you. Students in Oxford, Ohio, inspired by a program like Daily Bread in one of their hometowns, organized a food distribution program shuttling leftover food from the dining halls where they eat to the local New Life Mission, learning Ohio's Good Samaritan laws in the process.

Many people find opportunities for service arising from their work and professions. Work is what we do every day; it is often what is most familiar to us. Some of us may lobby for a more equitable work space; others may find that our professional talents can be used to help outside. Each of us knows what is calling and how we can answer.

A few years ago, Ben Cohen and Jerry Greenfield, the now famous makers of creamy Vermont ice cream, were becoming aware of the disappearance of the rain forests but were kept busy by their rapidly growing company. At the same time, Jason Clay, the executive director of Cultural Survival, was working on an agroforestry scheme; he hoped to introduce First World consumers to products that could be grown under the rain forest canopy in "extractive reserves," parts of the rain forest that could be farmed and thereby preserved. They met one night—the ice cream makers and the foundation head—and the idea of Rainforest Crunch was born. This cashew and Brazil nut brittle uses large quantities of nuts, which provide the forest people with three to ten times what they usually earn. And 40 percent of the profits from the candy go to rain forest–based preservation organizations, including Cultural Survival and the Rainforest Action Network.

Ben and Jerry have found a way to support endangered Amazonia right where they are—within the framework of their business. And, as is the way of creative ventures, it has continued to grow. As the nuts are prepared for the crunch, they give off "nut dust" at the rate of hundreds of pounds per week. Ben and Jerry began storing the dust, knowing it has nutritional value but not knowing what to do with it. Just as it threatened to overwhelm them ("Corporate Execs Buried in Nut Dust"), they conceived of the Rainforest Crunch Cookie, which could use the dust as flour. They had already proved that people will buy and eat sweets for a good cause, so they knew they had a market. And, to maximize the good effects, they connected with Bernie Glassman, abbot of the Zen Community of New York. The Zen Community had responded to the plight of the homeless in their area—Yonkers—by creating a holistic program that included job training at their Greyston Bakery. Ben and Jerry's idea was perfect—the Rainforest Crunch Cookies could not only give livelihood to Brazilian cooperatives and raise money for other rain forest preservation work but could generate jobs and training for homeless mothers in Yonkers. A stroke of compassionate genius. And it all happened right where everyone already was—at work.

Possibilities for compassionate action happen in every field. Sheldon Krimsky teaches in the Department of Urban, Social, and Environmental Policy at Tufts University. In the eighties he found himself part of a small group of people who were aware of many early developments in biotechnology, including biological weapons and gene manipulation. Reflecting on the negative impact of some of the developments in nuclear and chemical technologies, he recognized that these changes could have profound effects on people. He also knew that, without some translation and guidance, ordinary people would not have the information they needed to make intelligent decisions about them. So, with other concerned and public-spirited individuals, he formed the Council for Responsible Genetics, whose purpose is to educate and in fact protect the general public from possible negative effects of new discoveries. Their newsletter, *GeneWatch*, an extension of their professional work, covers important changes before they are discussed in the press. They have revealed research programs that would intensify chemical use in agriculture. They have discussed the army's plan to test extremely hazardous viruses in the form of aerosols to be used in warfare. And they have described "DNA fingerprints" and raised the question of who would have access to such data gathered by the police. This is not work they *have* to do. It comes from a feeling of responsibility and care for the rest of us who don't have access to this information. In the middle of their work, in their book-lined academic offices, they are acting from the heart.

In the medical profession there are, of course, many

opportunities for compassionate action; Wendy Orr was presented with a profound one. Wendy is a doctor in South Africa; in 1985, when the state of emergency was declared, she was a prison medical officer whose job was to examine detainees. She was expected to accept the regulation that no criminal or civil proceeding would be brought against members of the security forces for actions performed "in good faith" during the state of emergency. In other words, she was told to examine prisoners whom she found to have been systematically assaulted and abused after their arrest and be quiet about it. As a government doctor, she knew it would be very difficult for her if she spoke out, but she felt "morally and professionally bound" by what she saw to act. "Detainees were being subjected to various forms of torture and assault, including electric shocks; being forced to drink gasoline; being throttled or nearly suffocated with a wet towel; being slapped, kicked, whipped, punched, and beaten . . . having their heads banged against a wall, being jumped on while prone, and being forced to exercise to the point of exhaustion."

Despite attempts by her supervisors to stop her and to convince her of the validity of the regulation, Wendy felt she had to act. She says, "Unless I made a stand and did something about the plight of the detainees, I would be compromising my moral beliefs and my perception of my professional responsibility. My conscience told me that I could no longer stand by and do nothing." She filed an urgent application with South Africa's Supreme Court to restrain the police; in a remarkable move, the judge granted the restraining order, which was in effect until the temporary lifting of the state of emergency a year later. There is no way to know how much suffering Wendy prevented by her action.

She herself was ostracized by colleagues, her phone calls were monitored, she was prevented from seeing detainees, and eventually she was effectively pushed out of her position. But her only regret after it was all over was that "no district surgeons came out in my favor"; she was alone in her action.

Not all of us are in the immediate presence of such suffering as Wendy Orr was; some of us are. But everywhere there are ways to relieve suffering, and they can be part of our existing lives and responsibilities, not pulls away from them. They may just call us to change the way we are doing what we already do.

Do Your Homework

Believe those who are seeking the truth. Doubt those who find it.

André Gide

During the Second World War, families and friends sent American soldiers in Europe cartons of Lucky Strikes, which they thought were energizing and healthful as well as "free and easy on the draw." When nuclear power was first conceived, many people who are now avidly against its use campaigned for it, convinced that at last there was a problemless alternative power source that would free us from both black lung disease and dependence on Middle Eastern oil. As most of us know, things are often not what they seem. Sometimes the information that reveals the underside of an action or an issue is not yet available, but often it is. So before setting out on a goodwill mission or joining a social change organization, it's wise to do some research and reflection. It's good to do your homework.

Begin by reading and asking questions of anyone you

can find. Once you get just below the symptoms of suffering, there are subtleties and complexities that require thoughtful consideration. The problem is often not only what to change but how to change it. You won't solve all these issues in your mind at home, before starting to work with them, but if you educate yourself in this preliminary way, you will at least be aware of some of the questions.

With hunger, for example, even initial research will reveal that not only the solution but even the problem is paradoxical. As Frances Moore Lappé, cofounder of the Institute for Food and Development Policy, expresses it, "Hunger is needless. Everywhere. Sufficient food is produced globally to make us all overweight. Yet worldwide at least 700 million people suffer from hunger, and here in our own food-rich country, 20 million people go without adequate food." She says the challenging question is not "Why hunger?" but "Why do human beings allow decision-making power to concentrate in so few hands that hunger spreads, even among plenty?" She adds, "To work effectively to end hunger means first understanding why people are unable or feel unable to address its obvious roots. And then changing that reality."

When people are hungry, do you give them a meal or do you educate them? Progressive development agencies, such as Oxfam and World Neighbors, and thinkers, such as E. F. Schumacher, say teach people to farm or to work, because direct aid creates debilitating dependency, and development empowers. But what do you do when a hurricane destroys a crop and people are too hungry to learn and work? Is it harmful to feed people then? And what do you do in cities where people can't grow food and can't find work so that they can buy food? Do you feed them and create dependency, or help develop a job retraining program? Or, believing that food aid and job retraining are properly the work of the government, do you begin to advocate for legislative change or support litigation? Jim Tull, a member of a Catholic Worker house (one of many founded by Dorothy Day to give hospitality unconditionally to whoever comes to the door), expressed this tension as it arose for him:

"While it is strenuous indeed to feed 500 people at lunchtime when no more than 300 are expected, or to calm a psychotic shelter guest experiencing a severe reaction, it is more the constant balancing of objectives and the questioning of purpose and method that I have found most demanding.

"Common decency, in any tradition, tells us to feed a person who is hungry. The wisdom of this approach in its extreme has been debated over the Catholic Worker Movement's fifty-seven-year history. The tension is not so much over the appropriateness of providing for those who might be able to provide for themselves, although this question is often raised. The problem, I think, is that giving freely can have a disempowering effect over time on many of the recipients; it can foster dependence in general and can, for example, enable the diversion of resources into drugs and alcohol. Encouraging political action among the guests does not really compensate for this effect. . . . I wonder about the impact we are having."

Just when you thought working in a soup kitchen was a clear and simple form of compassionate action (which in fact it may be for you), it begins to look not so simple.

That's why it's helpful to do a little homework before you start and still be ready to act in the midst of uncertainty.

Working to relieve international hunger presents other dilemmas. What could be better than sending food to hungry children in poor countries, you wonder. Once you begin to ask some questions and read a little, you find out, however, that many of the agencies that distribute food internationally are working in cooperation with the U.S. Agency for International Development, which is in charge of all U.S. food aid. You find out that 90 percent of this food aid is not used for emergency famine relief. Most of what is given to foreign governments is sold by them to those among their people who can afford it; it is considered a form of supplemental income for the country and usually benefits the people in power more than the poor. Many world travelers know this from having been in Third World markets where rice or wheat is being sold from bags that say (in English, which most local people can't read), "A gift from the people of the United States."

You also discover that food aid often creates an appetite for food that cannot be produced locally; in Central America, for example, where corn is the native staple, people become accustomed to white bread when they are given food aid, and when the aid stops they continue buying wheat from the United States rather than growing more corn locally. You begin to wonder whether food aid, designed to help feed people, isn't in the long run making it more difficult for people to feed themselves. You may be confused, but you are beginning to ask some of the central questions. And when you begin to think and talk about these problems, you will be in a better position to find work that will both relieve immediate suffering and feel appropriate to you. And then the work will begin to answer the questions.

Such complex issues exist in every field where help and change are needed. Take, for example, the efforts of people trying to establish fair trade exchanges with Third World producers. It sounds fairly simple to buy crafts and other products from the Third World and sell them in the First World, thereby transferring some much-needed cash from place to place, establishing livelihood, reducing dependence on food aid, empowering the producers, and bringing beauty into industrialized lives. But, very soon you discover that "alternative trade" must be done with great care to be a helpful substitute for the open market. Before encouraging producers to invest in creating a production system and an inventory of goods, it is important to make sure that there will be continuing demand. In other words, if you are selling only to a local community of a limited number of people, after two or three seasons there may be no more demand for Nepalese rice paper stationery or Guatemalan place mats. Then the women who stopped planting their gardens in Nepal or Guatemala so that they could do woodblock printing or weaving are left without any income, and your goodwill and enthusiasm have created a mixed result.

Other questions come up as well in establishing fair trade opportunities: Do you sell whatever the local people produce, allowing them to maintain tradition and personal invention, or do you work with them to design a product that is more suitable for the North American or European market, so that their profit is more likely to be greater? Do you pay what you know to be a fair exchange for work, thereby making it harder to sell the products in a market where other importers have paid as little as they could? There will be hard times; are you willing to stay with producers and work through the problems of social or political unrest, bad harvests, family misfortunes, dishonesty? Obviously these are issues that only come to life once you are in the middle of the project, but it can be helpful to know as much as possible before you start.

Don't be discouraged. The good news is that we have access to a tremendous store of information about any field of interest, and there are many who have gone down each of these roads before us who will help us prepare. You can start by reading everything you can find about your subject: books, magazines, newspaper articles, organization brochures and newsletters. There's a short bibliography at the back of this book that may get you going; also visit libraries. Read the thinking on both (or many) sides of an issue. If you're not trained to use the library references (many are computerized now), ask the librarian for help. Visit bookstores too—if they don't have much on your subject, check *Books in Print,* which most bookstores have, and order what you want. Computer networks accessible through your home computer are good sources of information. PeaceNet, for example, has data bases of peace groups, speakers, foundations, and bibliographic, legislative, and project information; it also provides conferences, or specialized "bulletin boards," on subjects such as the international arms trade, companies that work in South Africa, food irradiation, green spirituality, and Rainforest Action groups.

Government agencies—local, state, and federal—are a great source of information on subjects from soil contamination and lead poisoning to current research on AIDS.

They gather and organize information, do data analysis, keep libraries, and publish periodicals, pamphlets, and books; many agencies have public information desks. You can call any of these agencies and ask them anything you need to know in their area of jurisdiction. They know where toxic dump sites are located, which diseases are more prevalent in which areas of the country, who owns what property, the ethnic balances of a neighborhood, and almost anything else factual that you want to know.

Check the yellow pages under "Community Organizations," "Foundations," "Human Services Organizations," "Peace Organizations," and "Social Service Organizations"; write or call those that are concerned with your interests, and ask for information.

Talk to everyone you can find who is interested in or has had experience in the field; the more directly involved a person is, the more useful will be his or her advice. Talk to people on both sides of the issues and on both sides of the need. If you want to work with teenage mothers, find some and ask what they think they need the most; program organizers may think that the young women should be separated from their mothers' influence; the young mothers may surprise you by saying that their mothers should also be part of the program. The head of a conservation society may tell you that buying and protecting the rain forest is what counts, but the Indians living under its canopy may say that finding a way for people to live within it and sustain it is the real need. Ask the hard questions, and listen carefully.

During gathering times like these, when you are acquiring great amounts of information, remember that it is easier to absorb if you allow yourself some mental spaciousness. Don't try to learn too much at once; go for walks or meditate during the process so that the information becomes integrated into your whole consciousness, not only your right brain. Some of the information will simply not make sense until you have actually started working and have had a little experience; don't worry, you'll know when you know. And some opportunities for action will simply feel more right than others, even if the information available seems to contradict your feeling. There are many levels of knowing; the homework is simply a process of getting in touch with information so that your choices will be more likely to relieve suffering.

Imagine

When life itself seems lunatic, who knows where madness lies? To surrender dreams . . . this may be madness. Too much sanity may be madness and, the maddest of all, to see life as it is and not as it should be.

DON QUIXOTE

During the Gulf War, Gregory Levey, aged twenty-one, walked onto the Common in Amherst, Massachusetts, set down a cardboard sign that said PEACE, stuffed his clothes with newspapers, poured paint thinner over his body, and set himself on fire. He died within two minutes. On that same day, Iraq had announced that there had been 20,000 Iraqi deaths so far in the war.

For some of us, it is a daily struggle to keep hope alive when our dream is of peace. Abbie Hoffman and Mitch Snyder both left us this message. It's hard to keep any dream alive that includes harmony and justice, even a dream that sees only the fulfillment of basic human needs for everyone in the greater family. But we need to do everything we can to keep these dreams alive, because the odds are against them. They are not something static, something to cling to; they are alive and changing, and we need to stay flexible and change with them.

Our dreams are the reason we act. Our visions of a better world give direction and meaning to our lives and our deaths. Keeping the dream alive keeps us alive, awake to our senses and our souls, to cold water, the underfoot crunch of a country road, the smell of summer honeysuckle, and the feeling of an open heart. We all have our vision of a world in which we'd like to live. When we are aware of this vision and yearn to bring it to life, compassionate action makes sense, right opportunities more often present themselves, and it is easier to be renewed when the dreams seem to have turned into nightmares.

Martin Luther King's dream still awakens us with its power: "I have a dream that one day men will rise up and come to see that they are made to live together as brothers. I still have a dream that one day the lion and the lamb will lie down together." His dream was inspired by the dream of Isaiah: "They shall beat their swords into plowshares, and their spears into pruning hooks; nation shall not lift up sword against nation, neither shall they learn war any more." And John Lennon's life and ours were inspired by his sweet dream: "Imagine no possessions, I wonder if you can. No need for greed or hunger, a brotherhood of man."

Dreams lead us to act with boldness and love. That they may be impossible dreams doesn't matter. They are not goals; they are the inspiration within each act as we move toward the vision. The cause and the effect, the means and the end, are not separate; they are one. We need to embrace the impossibility of achieving a world that has *no* suffering in it and yet work for change at the same time. The Buddhists say, "Sentient beings are numberless, and I vow to save them." How can this be? We find out only in the action.

Having such a dream doesn't mean that we should deny the present as it is; on the contrary, it means that we see things just as they are, including the obstacles and difficulties, yet act as if the realization of our dream is possible. It was because Martin Luther King, Jr., and Mohandas Gandhi knew their own hearts and the hearts of their people that they had their dreams. If Don Quixote had not had his dream, if he had let the rational skeptics around him take it from him, he would never have brought his loving-kindness and wisdom into the lives of the people of La Mancha or into our own. His vision came to life in his actions, and they revealed the hidden truth, which was filled with humor and joy.

Compassionate action is a way to keep the dream vital, present, breathing. If you need to get in closer touch with that dream, get out your handmade notebook or sit in front of your computer, and begin to put it into words. The words will be only a finger pointing at the moon, but they will help. Imagine that "better world" and what it would be like; it will tell you how to get there. Notice everything about it; if everyone in your perfect world has an automobile, and you begin to wonder how this could happen, you may learn a lot about the distribution of resources on the planet; if the grass in your vision world is green, you may be drawn to involvement in the development of alternative fuels, controls on toxic pesticides, or any of so many interrelated actions that will allow grass to continue to be green. Keep writing. Is everyone in this dream world getting enough to eat? How can this happen? Are there weapons systems? Does AIDS exist? Has the lion lain down with the lamb? Is color still a barrier that closes hearts and keeps people in prison? Every detail of your vision is important.

Lead with your dream. Let it be present in every act. It's what Gandhi was reminding us when he said, "Ask if your next act is of any value to the poorest person you know." That came from his dream. What will come from ours? Just imagine.

Stay Awake to Suffering

Do not close your eyes before suffering. Find ways to be with those who are suffering by all means, including personal contact and visits, images, sound. By such means, awaken yourself and others to the reality of suffering in the world.

GAUTAMA BUDDHA

This is the way Buddhist peace activist Thich Nhat Hanh understands the words of the Buddha on engagement. They are an important caution for us in the action-oriented, rush-for-results West. We need to find ways to be with one another, to be awakened to the reality of suffering and not be frightened or repulsed by it. We need to allow the suffering of others to become real for us, no matter how sad or angry we become. And we need to let that suffering help us look within ourselves for the subtle shadows of racism, sexism, all the "isms." We need to charge those "isms" to "wasms."

After visiting Guatemalan villagers and talking to young widows about their lives, Seva board members have found themselves in tears, sometimes for hours.

And they have felt anger—at the government for offering inadequate services, at the army for its brutal counterinsurgency, at the U.S. government for giving aid, at economic systems for creating the debt that takes the few resources of poor people, at themselves for not being able to stop the pain. But this is a necessary part of the process of opening up to suffering. Anything less is self-deception, that subtle state that keeps us from seeing things as they are and prevents us from changing them.

"Awaken yourself and others to the reality of suffering in the world." These words of the Buddha remind us that we need to open to the hard things as well as the easy ones. And we need to open wide—to go past ideas and headlines and concepts, right to the people who hurt. "Homelessness" as a concept does not exist on the street; what exists is Wendy, who used to make circuit boards for pay phones in Mississippi, until she lost her job and came north. Now Wendy lives in a Boston alley, four blocks from Lord & Taylor, with her friend Traveler. They drink wine and Listerine to get high, and eat Ragú spaghetti sauce or what they can find from the Dumpster. Among her cardboard bedclothes, Wendy has a stuffed brown gorilla named Henry. When we come to know Wendy the human being, not Wendy the idea or statistic, we can begin to appreciate her suffering. We need to do that if we are to discover how we can help.

The word *Buddha* comes from the root *buddh,* which means "awake." A Buddha is one who is awake. The historic Buddha, who lived 2,500 years ago, is said to have awakened through a process of inner exploration, which began when he left the protected environment in which he had been a young prince. Venturing out of the palace grounds one day, past the fragrant gardens and beyond the sheltering wall, he met village people and encountered suffering for the first time: he saw ordinary life, and with it he saw loneliness, sickness, old age, and death. Never having seen these before, he went through a radical change in his understanding of life. Touched by the pain, he began to look for a way to relieve it; he knew that the pain of others was his as well. He spent the rest of his life exploring suffering and the ways out of suffering; then he taught what he had learned, including the technique of meditation, to others.

We need to get out into our own twentieth-century villages (or cities), so that we can learn what is happening. We might hear words there, like these, which are from a Salvadoran peasant woman, words that wake us up to what is happening:

"I worked on the hacienda over there, and I would have to feed the dogs bowls of meat or bowls of milk every morning, and I could never put those on the table for my children. When my children were ill, they died with a nod of sympathy from the landlord. But when those dogs were ill, I took them to the veterinarian in Suchitoto.

"You will never understand violence or nonviolence until you understand the violence to the spirit that happens from watching your own children die of malnutrition." (From "Central America: The Right to Eat." San Francisco: Food First, 1988.)

As happened when the Buddha saw suffering, we are often changed once we hear such words. The Salvadoran mother's suffering becomes part of us. That is the beginning. We may have been aware of a problem such as homelessness or the malnutrition of Third World children, and may have been moved by it, but to be able to act effectively for change, to be able to search for solutions with passion and endurance we need to be in touch with the people who are hurting. We do not need to go through that greatest suffering of a parent—to watch our own children die—but we need to be close to mothers who have, we need to listen to their hopes and fears, and we need to get in touch with our own vulnerability in their presence.

Architects of social policy who have stayed in air-conditioned offices have rarely created programs that are well tuned to the needs of the poor or others who need their help. The World Bank, which reports from its headquarters in Geneva that "we know a great deal about who the poor are, and what must be done to improve their lives," is well known for projects such as the massive dam in the Narmada River valley in India, designed to improve water delivery and increase jobs in the area. The dam's huge reservoir will drown the farms and forests of 90,000 people, mostly tribal villagers. Although the bank says that the dam will improve agriculture and health, it doesn't seem to be what the local people want. Villagers such as Pem Singh, age thirty-seven, from Kakrana, are protesting: "I am against the Dam because it will make people miserable. Once one is uprooted from one's homeland, life becomes painful. We met with people who have been up-rooted from their village. Their cattle were dying due to lack of fodder. Many infants have died since they left their village. Now they want to move from the reset-tlement area."

In contrast, the great spokespeople for the suffering have been those who have spent time among them: Gan-dhi, who walked endlessly through the villages of India, talking to the poor; Martin Luther King, Jr., who lis-tened to the black community from Montgomery to Memphis; Mother Teresa, who chose the streets of Cal-cutta over the refuge of the monastery; liberation theo-logian Gustavo Gutiérrez, who lived among the poor of Rímac, a slum of Lima, Peru; Brazilian union leader Chico Mendes, who organized the rubber tappers of Acre to save the fragile ecosystem of Amazonia; and Rachel Carson, who lived with the land and became one of the first voices to warn us of the suffering of the earth.

Chilean novelist Ariel Dorfman, who has lived and worked "wandering on the boundaries of development" with the Mataco aborigines of the El Chaco jungle in Argentina, told a story in *Direct to the Poor* that reminds us how little we often know about one another:

"As a child, one of my friends thought the Matacos were some sort of animal. He had been brought up on a sugar mill in the province of Tucumán, where at night the adults would tell stories. One story dealt with some-thing called the Matacos, which were hunted down by the hundreds in the jungles of the Gran Chaco forest. He remembered, above all, an evening when a guest of his father related how Matacos had been picked off one by one by soldiers from the back of a moving train. This confirmed his impression that the victims were monkeys or wild beasts.

"That idea persisted until several years later. One morning he went out into the yard and saw his grandmother standing in front of two small, bronze-faced children, an impassive brother and sister. With a pair of large scissors, she began to shear off their black, dirty hair. 'These Matacos,' she announced, 'are full of lice. This is the only way to get rid of them.' "

"It was then that my friend realized that the Matacos were Indians."

Before we can respond to one another's needs with integrity, we have to get to know one another. All of our suffering comes from the same source, but in each of us it is expressed differently. Following the lead of the Buddha and Gandhi, we need to be where the suffering is. We need to know its texture and quality; we need to hold the babies in our arms. There are many ways to do this, but the goal is the same: proximity, familiarity, dialogue, relationship. Jesus, as the Son of God, presumably could have chosen any life circumstance for his time on earth; he chose to be born to a poor carpenter and his wife and to live among the poor, the sick, the blind, the lame, and prostitutes. He taught by example; only when you know a situation well can you discover the ways in which it can be changed.

Here are some suggestions for learning before you act. If you are drawn to the people of Central America, visit your local Central American support group. Ask to meet refugees living in your area; talk with them about their lives at home and their lives here, about their struggles and their hopes, their culture and their children. Volunteer to teach English or help with childcare or guide people through government bureaucracies. Travel to Central America with a group such as Habitat for Humanity, which offers the opportunity to build houses in Honduras. Or study Spanish in a school such as Casa Romero in Guatemala City, which will place you with a Guatemalan family during your stay. Or take an educational tour with a group such as Center for Global Education, having a theme such as health care or human rights; you can visit both cities and villages and learn from the people there about their country.

If you want to work on problems here at home, volunteer to work in a food pantry or soup kitchen and talk with people about their lives and how they got there. With a friend, spend a night on the street and see what it's like; in New York, you will learn that street sleepers leave out a little food for the rats to keep them from running around during the night. Volunteer to answer a hot line for runaway teenagers, for child abusers, for drug users, for the lonely and frightened. Visit a prison; arrange to talk to prisoners about their lives there and the conditions outside that contributed to their being there. Be an AIDS buddy. Volunteer to help in a hospital ward for AIDS babies. Sit through a day in an inner-city school; talk to kids and to teachers. Accompany a social worker; talk with the families she visits. Visit a farm family that has faced foreclosure; give support and listen.

There is a favorite children's story about the process

of coming to know one another. It is about a velveteen rabbit stuffed with sawdust who was often snubbed by the other, more expensive toys. One day he asked his friend, the old, wise, experienced Skin Horse,

"What is REAL? . . . Does it mean having things that buzz inside you and a stick-out handle?"

"Real isn't how you are made," said the Skin Horse. "It's a thing that happens to you. When a child loves you for a long, long time, not just to play with, but REALLY loves you, then you become Real."

"Does it hurt?" asked the Rabbit.

"Sometimes," said the Skin Horse, for he was always truthful. "When you are Real you don't mind being hurt."

"Does it happen all at once, like being wound up," he asked, "or bit by bit?"

"It doesn't happen all at once," said the Skin Horse. "You become. It takes a long time. That's why it doesn't often happen to people who break easily, or have sharp edges, or who have to be carefully kept."

Like the velveteen rabbit, we don't become real for one another right away—it takes time and being together before there is an opening for the love that makes us real for one another. Being together in service can give us that.

Carolyn North, of Daily Bread in Oakland/Berkeley, sees these opportunities as a central part of the work: "Many of the volunteers form very special relationships with the people at the shelters. The woman who does the Wednesday pickup from Ramona's Restaurant, for example, decided to have her birthday party at the shelter. She said, 'I realized that these were the people I wanted to be with.' Generally these are people who would not ordinarily meet each other. But there's not a sense of 'we' and 'they' but rather a sense that we're all in this together. It has to do with sharing and not charity."

When Peter Lombardi, formerly volunteer coordinator of the Hospice at Mission Hill in Boston, was assigned his first hospice patient, it was Tony. Tony, an Italian housepainter who had lived a fairly typical working-class life in the Northeast, was dying of cancer. Peter remembers, "I was intimidated by Tony and the concept of who Tony was. I felt ill prepared. I had done the hospice training, but I didn't feel equipped to deal with a dying person whom I didn't know. . . . But what I thought I needed to do with someone so different from me was not what I really needed to do at all. All I needed to do was be myself. All I needed to offer is what I offer every day to anyone I come across. Just to respect this man."

When compassion arises, we see that we are interconnected, and we feel the pain of others as our own. As we grow to appreciate that unity, we also need to remember the absolute wonder of our differences. We need to learn the texture and quality of one another's lives. We cannot always actually walk, as the Native Americans say, in another person's moccasins to learn her or his suffering, but we can walk together in a spirit of friendship, witness, support, and love. We can be allies for each other. We can remind ourselves that suffering is something familiar to us all. From that awakened spirit can come dialogue, exploration, and, at its best, compassionate action. So stay awake to suffering; get closer to people who are different from you in their race, culture, language, religion, and sexual preference. As Emily Dickinson said, "Who hears may be incredulous; who witnesses, believes."

Work Alone or With Others

All of us are interdependent. Whether we realize it or not, each of us lives eternally in the red.

MARTIN LUTHER KING, JR.

We may want to clean up the River Ganges, bring peace to the Middle East, or wake up the Democratic Party, but, whatever we do, we need to choose between working alone and working with others. We usually have some preferences based on experience, but take a few moments here to consider the differences between working alone and working with others.

Although most compassionate action happens in relationship with others, sometimes the relationship is not physical and immediate. Certain work can only be done alone, even if we are working to benefit other people. Many artists work alone, then perform their work in public. Allen Ginsberg was alone when he wrote the poem "White Shroud," about his dream of his mother, Naomi, abandoned in an alleyway in "her moth-eaten rabbit fur hat." Later he read it aloud to 5,000 people from the pulpit of the Cathedral of St. John the Divine in New York City at a benefit for the homeless.

When grass-roots activist Fran Peavey discovered she was HIV positive as a result of a nearly forgotten blood transfusion, she spent time by herself keeping a rigorously honest journal of her fear, isolation, anxiety, and sadness. The writing turned into a courageous and loving action for others when, with the encouragement of her friends, she decided to publish it. She said, "The decision to publish was not an easy one. It is tough to be so vulnerable in print. . . . I am embarrassed by my prejudice . . . and by my uncaring attitude toward friends of mine who suffered early in the history of the disease." Fran decided to turn her private writing into a public act because she wanted to share with others what had been so painful for her to learn.

Sometimes when we see what needs to be done, we just get up and do it. Sometimes that happens when we are alone. Mother Wright, known as the Angel of the Poor, feeds the homeless in an Oakland park. Several days a week she just starts chopping the celery and onions and preparing the batter for the chicken. If people arrive to help, she puts them to work. If they don't, she does it all herself. If her sons are there between painting jobs to load the heavy pans into her van, they do. If they're not, she does it alone. She is used to being with people—she had thirteen children—but her style is to go forward herself and let others be drawn to her, as they are. She says that God is always there.

Even if a project involves others later, we may start out alone. It may need a time of investigation before it becomes a plan for action. We may need to reflect and study, to "do our homework." A good deal of that work is naturally done alone.

Some years ago, rock musician Little Steven (Stevie Van Zandt) gave a talk in Cambridge, Massachusetts, where there was an active movement to persuade Harvard University to divest itself of its holdings in South Africa. Little Steven showed a film about the making of his protest song and video, "Sun City." Many people were asking, "What can I do? How can I help?" He related how he had gone to South Africa, asking those very questions, ready to "join up," to give his energy to ending apartheid. His South African friends appreciated his fervor and support but told him to go home, find out everything he could about apartheid, including the United States's involvement in it, then look at his own life and talents and see how they could be used for change. This he did. He returned, he studied, he talked to people, he looked at his life. The result was a project that involved many people: a song and video that explained his belief that cooperating with the South African government, even through providing entertainment for the white elite, was supporting their policy of apartheid. The project involved Steven's rock star friends, communicated in the way that he knew best, and linked the problem abroad with the one at home. It started with one person's questioning and study.

Working alone, we may have more time for reflection. We may be better able to work at our natural pace. We may feel safer in ways that help us take risks. Solitude may give us the space we need for artistic expression. And it can be a balance for the time we spend with others, allowing us to hear our own truth more clearly. Working alone is right for some of us some of the time. If we listen, we know when that is.

At other times, action in groups has a strong draw. Anyone who has been part of an inspired demonstration, such as a protest against nuclear weapons or a candlelight walk for women's rights, knows the exhilaration of being part of something larger than oneself, united with others for a cause. Even baking whole wheat rolls in a shelter kitchen or organizing an office to recycle its computer paper, people have experienced the satisfaction that comes from being part of community working for change. This basic sharing of space and purpose can remind us of the simple truth that we are all members of the world community, here to help one another on our common journey home.

Working in groups has the advantage of fulfilling our yearning for community. Many of us in the white mainstream of this country come from dysfunctional, nonnurturing, unloving families. Our rituals and traditions are largely gone, and our sense of belonging has weakened; the emphasis in our culture on competition and individual achievement has eroded our sense of community and solidarity. No longer tribal, we still need support, loving care, and interaction with a variety of other human beings; as is better know among other subcultures, it is rare for a single relationship or the nuclear family to satisfy all human needs.

We see attempts to reconstruct the extended family in new ways all around us. In the film of the Amnesty International concert tour Human Rights Now, the English rock musician Sting walks off a plane in Chile and into the arms of one after another of the Mothers of the

Disappeared, for whom he had written the poignant song "They Dance Alone." The image is powerful; it seems to celebrate a reunion of spirit, a return to the mother. Later we see him dancing with each of them in their white kerchiefs while Bruce Springsteen sings—each of these weary, heavy, lonely women becomes young and lithe, smiling as she whirls. Ah, to be part of the family.

Compassionate action can help heal our feelings of separation and loss. Because of its intimate nature, committed as it is to the development of trust, respect, dialogue, dignity, and cooperation, it is related to our search for affinity in some special ways. It acknowledges not only our interconnection but also our interdependence. Yes, it says, we need one another, and, furthermore, we are ready to acknowledge that fact and start acting on it. And when this action happens amid suffering, it can awaken a tenderness of heart from which we feel both love and nurturance. For example, the bond that develops between a dying person and a friend can nurture life. Francis Giambrone, who in his AIDS support work has been close to many who have died, told about one who touched him deeply:

"There were powerful, poignant, touching moments when Tom realized he was dying, when he would talk about dying, when he was scared of it, when he was afraid that all his work was for naught. He owned that he was dying, he worked on the dying process, and he pulled me totally into it. He would ask questions, and he would force me to think about things I hadn't thought about. He was scared, but he could talk about it. And he let me be scared with him.

"One night I was vacationing in Mexico. I knew his

death was close when I left him, but with AIDS you never know. It could be tomorrow, it could be two years from now. I'll never forget that night—I woke up in the middle of the night screaming and crying and sweating. I called home right away—did Tom die? He hadn't died that night, but he had told everyone that he wanted no support, no more IVs, and that he wanted to die. It was strange, but it felt good, as though I had in some way been there with him. . . . It was a spiritual journey with another human being that I'd never had before."

We are awakened not only in the solitude of prayer, meditation, and reflection but also by being with one another. *Compassion* actually means "suffering with," and when that is happening, when we need one another's help, we are sometimes more likely to awaken. The white college students who became part of Mississippi Summer in 1964 were radically changed by their relationships with the black students of CORE and SNCC and the people of Mississippi. They saw American life from a new perspective, and they saw some of their own relative conditioning and their fears and prejudices. They returned to the North with a new understanding and a sense of mission that affected the entire civil rights movement in the following years.

We are looking for ways to help and yearning for growth in ourselves, and we often find both of these in community, in the presence of others. If we are lonely or simply stuck in our ways of perceiving and acting, we may find warm welcome and creative challenge to our fixed ideas. In Seva, board members often say they trust the group mind more than their own. This doesn't mean that many excellent ideas don't come from individual people, but it does mean that our individual perspectives can be challenged and enriched by the ideas and support of others.

Jean Vanier, a Frenchman of privilege and wealth who turned his back on a life of security to work with the handicapped in France, founded l'Arche (or Ark) communities—familylike settlements where the handicapped and nonhandicapped share their lives. L'Arche is committed to "the sacredness of the individual, the centrality of the human heart, and the joy that arises when we begin to perceive a handicap as a 'blessed weakness'—a path to compassion, understanding, and spirituality." Vanier says of being nourished by his work:

"Sometimes the greatest resource of all can be a small gesture of kindness. It is often a gentle look from someone who is vulnerable that relaxes us, touches our heart, and reminds us of what is essential. One day I went with some sisters of Mother Teresa to a slum in Bangalore, where they looked for people with leprosy. The sores stank, and, humanly speaking, it was revolting. But the people there had light in their eyes. All I could do was hold the instruments the sisters were using, but I was glad to be there. The expressions and smiles of the people seemed to reach right into me and renew me. When I left, I felt an inexplicable joy, and it was they who had given it to me. I remember too an evening in a prison in Calgary, Canada, where I spent three hours with the members of Club 21—the men who are serving more than twenty-one years for murder. They touched me and recharged my spirit. They changed something in me."

Many groups have emerged to help answer the need for service through community, including church groups;

communes and other group living situations; solidarity groups; nonprofit organizations committed to a particular cause; support groups of various kinds, including the fast-growing twelve-step network; growth centers; political parties; travel groups; and spiritual life centers. Or you may find that the most natural group in which to become an activist is your own family. Working together to create change in the world and to relieve the suffering of others can be bonding and refreshing to a family. It can be more rewarding than the usual pastimes. In a busy family, it can be the impetus that gets family members to commit time to doing something together.

Patti and Tom Pierce live in Gloucester, Massachusetts, with their two young children. Tom is a family doctor who spends a great deal of time with his patients. Patti helps run the office and is studying for her master's degree in social work. At a summer retreat, Tom saw a slide show about the life of the Mayan Indians in Guatemala, and, although their life was already very full, he decided he wanted to help. Gloucester is a port where artists live among fishermen. In this place, Tom and Patti wondered whether they could find something artistic that would benefit the Mayans, who love beauty so much. After enlisting support from friends, Tom and Patti started the "annual T-shirt offering," a premium sent to supporters who make donations to Seva's Guatemala project through the Gifts of Service catalog. The T-shirts increased the appeal of the fund-raiser, engaged many local people, and helped keep the situation of the Mayan people alive in many people's minds.

As Patti said, "Working together is great for support. I was more skeptical than Tom about whether it could work, so Tom did the initial legwork, finding someone who could do the first drawing. Then, when I saw the shirt, it lit a fire in me, and I thought, Well, I'd really like to paint. That back and forth continued. When my energy wanes, he picks up the slack for a while. It's wonderful to feel empowered together, to discover together that we can help. And of course we saw our differences too. For me the hands-on work of painting and working with other people was nurturing, rewarding. Tom has been more the idea person, so he hasn't gotten that."

As we struggle to bring about a peaceful and livable planet for the next generations, it seems obvious that it is good to involve the children in the process. Tom and Patti are looking for ways to expand the T-shirt project to include their children, perhaps with something made by the children themselves that could be used in the catalog, or something that could be made by their children and their friends to be sent directly to children in Guatemala. Other families have done recycling projects together, delivered meals with their children, walked for hunger, written to politicians, helped with day care in local shelters, studied causes of poverty here and around the world. The EarthWorks Group published a small treasure that can be used by families called 50 *Simple Things Kids Can Do to Save the Earth.*

Tim Gilbert is a playground planner and parks designer in Ann Arbor, Michigan. When his close friend Scott and Scott's young daughter died in a car accident, Tim designed a memorial playground that could be constructed almost entirely by unskilled volunteers, including children. Many families met on four Saturdays and worked, laughed, and cried together. When it was over, Ann Arbor had a new park, and Tim and many others, including the children, had created a monument of family love to his friend.

Of course, whether you begin by working alone or in community, there will be difficulties. Compassionate action is, after all, part of life, and many wise beings, from the Buddha to Woody Allen, have reminded us that life is inseparable from suffering. Working alone can bring loneliness and boredom. You can become self-righteous. You can lose touch with the larger social picture; you may need reality checks. And working in community with others reveals other things: in many ways it is not as safe as a room of one's own. Limitations and attachments become obvious. You may discover emotional weaknesses, inability to get on with other people, desires for personal gratification, or impatience and arrogance. You may at times feel incapable of loving. Working with the poor and homeless, you may develop a haunting desire for a bigger and more expensive place to live. You might disapprove of a board member's life-style and find yourself unwilling to listen to her proposal for a new project. Because you desire a team member sexually, you may overlook his incomplete contribution to the team.

But these challenges are what Tibetan teacher Chögyam Trungpa called "the manure for our growth." Seeing the truth in ourselves is part of the process of developing insight: as we grow, not only do we develop empathy for others who act in the same unconscious ways but we have the opportunity to change our behavior so that it resonates with the principles we value and are working for. Since our lives are our message, the more peaceful and generous we become in our interactions, the more likely we are to help create peace and generosity in the wider spheres of our influence. And working on oneself, of course, fits within the guidelines for compassionate action: we can start small, work right where we are, do something clearly within our own power, and be of benefit to the whole. And when we work on our problems in the presence of others and the suffering of the world, we are less likely to get lost in the endless mirrors of narcissism. Change is a gradual and continual process. Whether our compassionate action is done alone or in a group, inner exploration remains the complement to external action, and, with time and patience, it can lead to clearer awareness, action with more integrity, and a freer flow of the heart's breath.

Reflect on Your Motives

Knowing others is wisdom; knowing the self is enlightenment.

TAO TE CHING

You cross the street to avoid looking in the eyes of a homeless woman. Your heart is calling, but you don't respond. Why? Maybe it's because you learned not to be vulnerable as a child. You became afraid to be who you are, afraid to listen to your heart. It's too dangerous. Opening to this homeless woman, even for a moment of eye contact, may make you feel vulnerable as you become aware of what she needs and what you have. Questioning the status quo, however fleetingly, may seem just too difficult at this moment; your conditioned response may be to cross the street and avoid vulnerability. You haven't consciously thought these things, but you have made an unconscious decision, one of so many moments in an urban day. You pass on to buy the paper or get some lunch before going to your meeting.

This is us living the busy and unexamined life, acting

from that complex of motives that takes us through the day. But when we don't pay full attention to our inner dialogue, to our feelings and thoughts, and we don't answer the call of the heart, we feel alienated from ourselves and from life around us, however subtly, and we don't experience the moment as fully as we might. As we pass by the homeless woman, life passes us by.

Compassionate action gives us an opportunity to wake up to some of our motives and to act with more freedom. It gives us the chance to put ourselves out on the edge, and if we are willing to take a clean look at what we see there, we can come to know ourselves better. We can't, of course, change what is arising in us at any moment, because we can't change our pasts and our childhoods. But when we listen to our own minds and stop being strangers to ourselves, we increase the number of ways we can respond to what arises. Then we know when we are resisting contact with a poor person because of something that happened in childhood, and we know that now we have nothing to fear either from the homeless person or from the examination of our place in the economic structure. We are here right now, and we are free. We can either walk past the person, talk to her, give her some money, and go on, maybe reflecting on the causes of homelessness and its relation to our hot tub, or we can cross the street because we are still carrying around fear and protection from childhood and don't want to deal with it today on the way to a meeting. Whichever we do, with increasing awareness comes an appreciation of our actions as they are, and then they begin to change. Even if we haven't acted compassionately toward the street woman, we haven't repressed the fact that she exists, and we aren't judging ourselves; as awareness and acceptance increase, not blocked by our fears, we tend to act more humanely. It happens naturally.

A central quality in people who are drawn to compassionate action is empathy for those who need help, a commonality with people who are suffering, oppressed, or vulnerable. This feeling is often a result of imprinting during childhood, when we had no control over what was happening and felt frightened, helpless, vulnerable, sick, and alone in bed on a summer night. A friend who works with refugees lived through a middle-class childhood with a violent alcoholic father. She carries an image of herself and her two young sisters, huddled, waiting for the fighting inside their house to be over, feeling small, unprotected, and powerless to change anything. When she grew up, she found herself identifying intimately with those who felt helpless in the face of outside forces— battering husbands, uncaring governments, or mysterious diseases such as AIDS—even if there was nothing else in their lives that overlapped with hers. She found herself drawn away from a successful career in business toward work in which she could help people take responsibility for their own lives.

Empathy allows us to feel at home with people we don't know and closer to people we do know. It can encourage us to do many useful things, because we tend to act from inside another person's shoes. But we have to be careful about even such good qualities when they are developed through early experiences, especially traumatic experiences. They can cause trouble when we act out of feelings that grew along with the compassion. If your empathy began to develop when you were seven and felt powerless to stop your father from drinking or hitting your mother, unless you are aware of this fact you may start acting as though you were seven again while you are working with others who are somehow vulnerable. While you are working with refugees on the U.S. border, for example, your own seven-year-old anger at your parents may become so intermixed with your disapproval of a government that isn't caring for these people that you overlook ways in which you could work with the government for the refugees' benefit.

Ravi Khanna, former Oxfam America campaigns director, said, "It is so important to ask why you are doing social action. In organizations, it is often too hot a question for people. There is the danger of not agreeing with each other, so you don't discuss it. Sometimes it takes a crisis to push the issue—at Oxfam, the Ethiopia famine, which expanded our work considerably, pushed it for us. It was good, but it was very difficult."

The reason to look at motives that developed in the past is that we want to act more consciously now. We don't want to pass on our own insecurities in a new form to those with whom we are working and thus create more confusion. Of course, it is a long and gradual process, learning to act from full awareness, but accepting that motives are there and looking at them as best we can is a good first step.

Some people, of course, spend large parts of their lives trying to identify deeply hidden motives, through therapy, meditation, group support, and other practices. Such an intensive process is not necessary before becoming involved in compassionate action; compassionate action is itself a process that reveals motivation. But as you are getting ready to start, try this exercise to stimulate your awareness. It is a spiritual as well as psychological exercise; that is, it poses that favorite question of the great Indian saint Ramana Maharshi, whose students asked themselves constantly, "Who am I?" The repetition allows the answers to keep changing. In this context, ask the question, "Why do I want to do this?"

Let's take development work in Guatemala. "Why do I want to go to Guatemala to work with the widows and children?" "Well, I have been living my life mainly for myself and my family; this will make me feel better about myself." That may work until you begin to see the complexity of the task, and you glimpse just how insidious Third World poverty is, and you realize that your actions—such as giving people food directly instead of teaching them farming techniques that would enable them to be independent and feed themselves—may have hurt more than they helped. You see that the food may have created dependency and the degraded sense of self-worth that goes with it. You no longer feel entirely good about yourself: "I shouldn't have gotten into this without knowing more about it." However, since you have now started to understand the situation and may eventually be able to make a positive contribution, this is the time to look for a deeper level of motivation, a new reason to keep going.

The shadow side of self-gratification is guilt, one of the great American motivators. Those of us growing up in the Judeo-Christian tradition were given considerable support both for feeling guilt and for acting out of it. Guilt is often experienced as a vague but haunting sense of having done something wrong or, more seriously, of being something bad. Guilt is related to a number of things, from feeling the weight of original sin to discovering that you are gay in prep school during the 1940s. It dissolves when we begin to realize who we are through meditation or life experience, but much of the time it is too much with us, and the antidote is often thought to be "doing good."

Guilt, as any motivation, may lead us to do some wonderful work. In Guatemala, guilt over being part of the United States, which is providing money and guns to the police and the military, who have been accused of violating the human rights of the people, causes many "gringos" to try to redress the balance by supporting communities who are recovering from the violence. But guilt can veil the truth and contribute to exhaustion. It can prevent us from acting with balance. When accompanied by anger, as it often is, guilt can prevent the gentler qualities of kindness and appreciation from being present in our work. Guilt about the homeless on the New York streets led one woman to work long hours at a job she hated in a soup kitchen, where she came to resent the very people she had hoped to serve. In the long run, guilt, as does self-gratification, often turns out to be unsatisfying as a motivator. We need to go deeper.

"Why do I want to do this?" Beyond the personal motives of self-gratification and guilt, we have social motives: "Other people will think I am a good person for doing this. This work reflects the values of my family, church, or friends." Could be, and that might keep us recycling while others are watching, or it might lure us onto boards of directors or school committees. An exceptional need to be approved (perhaps as a residue of an unhappy childhood or an alcoholic family) might drive us to give a major part of our energy to a truly worthwhile task. With the Guatemala support work, the need for approval wears thin when the work becomes incredibly absorbing and you notice that your friends are equally busy with their lives and aren't really noticing what you are doing. Working for development groups pays so little that some friends actually become disapproving; they wonder why you are not being more responsible financially, why you are late paying bills or unable to vacation with them. And then—as you get deeper into it—people who were in support of helping Guatemala begin to question your methods. Your radical friends say that any development work makes village people feel a little bit better, just enough so they won't challenge the root causes of their poverty, which are social and political; your conservative friends say that improving health among the poor only increases the birthrate and causes more unemployment, scarcer resources, and more suffering. "Hey, I started to do this so that other people would approve. What happened?" We need to go deeper still.

"Why do I want to do this? What is the truth? What about those times when I felt love for all beings? Don't all people deserve to have their basic needs satisfied and to enjoy freedom? I am unhappy when I am not feeling clear about how and why to help. I want my actions to reflect my deepest inner understanding."

When our hearts open, when we know that we are in fact the world, when we experience the pain of others in our own blood and muscle, we are feeling compassion. It begins as gentle love and acceptance of ourselves, and it extends to include our family and friends and, eventually, all beings, those we know and those we do not, as well as all of nature—rocks and raccoons and stars and water. We begin to reflect that, although the suffering of others may not be our fault, it *is* our responsibility, not in a heavy sense of having the world on our individual shoulders but in a natural way, as if we were all part of the same body; if there is an itch, we scratch it; if one part of it hurts, we try to heal it.

We also begin to understand that everyone wants to be happy, all of us, everywhere—the vulnerable and oppressed among us as well as the militant and oppressive. We would all like to eat when we are hungry and sleep without fear when we are tired, to do work that is productive and satisfying, to honor the spirit each in our own way, to watch our children grow up in a healthy and peaceful place. By acting compassionately, by helping to restore justice and to encourage peace, we are acknowledging that we are all part of one another.

When we are motivated by compassion, by acceptance and love of one another, we are also more likely to stay with the work even when it is difficult. Through doing this, we learn to respect the process of long-term learning, and we discover that learning happens through dialogue, mutual exploration, and respect for one another's strengths and weaknesses. Helping ceases to be one person doing something to or for another; it becomes circular; the helper and the helped and the action itself are all part of a seamless whole.

When Carolyn North began Daily Bread to collect food from bakeries and restaurants for food pantries and soup kitchens, she found that she often needed to remind herself that each of us has a role in the Big Picture and that attitudes and opinions that separate us arise only too easily. "What I'm trying to do is manifest this spiritual connection on the level of community, by actively bringing people together and sharing. It's an attempt to get people in the community to rebalance something that has gone very out of balance. But one thing I had to face pretty early was the dilemma of self-righteousness. We were often tempted to judge a fancy restaurant when we picked up twenty pounds of surplus salmon—that there's something immoral about such an operation, that we were better than they were. At first I didn't recognize it as a problem, and then I realized that we are all doing our part in the community."

This appreciation of all parts of the whole helps us begin to feel what it is to be an instrument rather than a maker of change. Mother Teresa is said to have given this advice to a monk who said he loved lepers and wanted to work only with them. That meant that he didn't want to do chores that he considered less important. "Your vocation," she said, "is not to serve the lepers. It is to belong to Jesus. Your work is the means to put your love for him into action, but your vocation is to belong to Jesus." The act itself is not as important as the spirit in which you do it. The brother is said to have changed completely. It no longer mattered whether he was cooking, washing streets, or taking care of the lepers. Whether we appreciate that story as a Christian teaching or hear Mother Teresa's reference to Christ as a metaphor for the truth within us, the message is the same: when we are motivated by love and compassion, we become instruments for what needs to be done, and the work becomes more joyful and more satisfying.

"Why do I want to do this?" It's a big question, the answer keeps changing, and sometimes you'll feel like saying, "Who cares, forget the endless self-absorption, I just want to get it done." Certainly, the goal is not to be rationally conscious at every moment of why you are acting; in true compassionate action, in fact, we tend to lose ourselves entirely into the work, becoming one with the service and the person being served. As in meditation, we are simply and naturally present, acting in a relaxed rather than a studied, intellectual way. But asking ourselves this question will help us become more aware of who we are; it will help us act more consciously. Remember that no answer is absolute. Trying to define yourself, as Alan Watts said, is like trying to bite your own teeth. But the answers will provide some pieces of the puzzle of how to make space for compassion to arise and how to act on it when it does, and these pieces may help relieve the suffering of others and allow our own selves to be whole. Many people before Mother Teresa have held poor and dying babies, but we are drawn to her because there is something in the way she moves and looks that reminds us that we and the baby are one. Such conviction and example help restore the balance for which we and the world are yearning.

Resources, Skills, and Talents

It's all done with people.

WAVY GRAVY

In the mountains of Sierra los Cuchumatanes in north-west Guatemala, a meeting was beginning. Many people from the community had come, especially those who were the official representatives of the many small *aldeas,* or hamlets, within the community. The meetinghouse was made of adobe and had a tin roof, which was cheaper and easier to install than the traditional thatch. Inside the room were some simple pine chairs and two long, narrow benches; on the wall were a picture of the Sacred Heart of Jesus and a calendar advertising chemical fertilizer. The people were all Mayans, descendants of the people who gave us corn, the number zero, the Mayan calendar, and the Tikal pyramids. They had recently returned to their village after two years of hiding from the army, which had threatened to kill them during the violence of the early eighties. Now they were about to meet for the first time with some people from the North, who might help them with a development project.

Don Benito opened the meeting with a welcome to the visitors and with thanks to God. Then he began to talk about the situation: "Our houses were burned, our animals died, our land is fallow. Many of our men were killed. We have no tools, no seeds, no fertilizer. We have nothing. We are only humble campesinos."

Three years later, the people Don Benito had called humble, by which he meant useless, not modest, had created a healthy, productive community, with good harvests, a medical program, houses for even the widows and orphans, a weaving and tailoring project, and a library. All they had received from the outside was training and some cash to prime the pump. Overwhelmed by their needs, they had greatly understated their talents and resources: they knew how to grow corn, they knew how to build houses, they knew which herbs reduce pain and which flowers attract bees; they had a deeply internalized sense of community, which encouraged cooperation and increased productivity, and they were open to learning new skills, such as tailoring and preventive health care. They already had everything they needed, except a small amount of help from the outside.

We often underestimate ourselves when we think about what our resources are; we become "humble campesinos." But each of us has something valuable to offer the world. When thinking about how to help, we need to look at and appreciate what we have and who we are, including skills, talents, money, time, and other resources. If we take an unbiased look at ourselves (difficult as that is), we will find that, in spite of all our limitations and neuroses, each of us knows a healing herb or a farming technique or simply loves to hold babies —we all have something to contribute to the healing of the whole. It may not be glamorous or seem important, but don't overlook it: we are all in this ark for a reason.

Don't be afraid to acknowledge the obvious: you understand things about children because you are a mother. Of course, you think, I know how to get kids to wear their red mittens when they want to wear the green ones, but that's not a skill. It's just who I am. That's it—that's what we have to give, who we are. And if someone had helped George Bush and Saddam Hussein be a little more relaxed about their mittens, we might have avoided a lot of suffering in the Persian Gulf. So it helps to acknowledge everything that we are. We are much more than we think, and it is often those overlooked aspects of ourselves that can make a difference for someone else.

It can be useful to make a description of yourself: who you are and what you have to offer. Write it as a list or write it as your life story. Find a comfortable space and some paper and write the first draft for yourself, so you can do it without thinking about others reading it. Let it flow: put down whatever comes into your mind; surprise yourself. Include that college summer job when you worked in the basement of the Metropolitan Museum addressing catalogs or the time you worked for Sam Pino's Amusements putting up carnival rides. Then make a second draft to show to other people. Include the usual defining information, such as your age, sex, formal education, and employment, but remember to include anything else that may seem interesting about you. Here are three examples:

I once lived in a Buddhist monastery in India, meditating from early morning till late at night. I shared a small cement room with one other woman, and we didn't eat after noon. I learned to live with very little.

I was born late into my family, and my parents and aunts and uncles were all very old. I became very comfortable around old people.

I was born in the Dominican Republic. I came to New York as a kid, and I was the only person on the block who spoke English. I went to hospitals a lot to help people with translating and to figure out how things worked. I suppose you could say I was developing advocacy skills.

Now make a comprehensive list of your skills and talents. If you've been driving all your adult life, you may forget that driving is an asset for a food collection program that needs people to take day-old bread from a bakery to a soup kitchen. If you manage a department for Digital Equipment, remember to tell the AIDS Action Committee that you know how to use Lotus 1-2-3 and can create a financial statement—they might need just that skill. If you can cut hair, play the piano, speak another language, cook, paint signs, or deliver babies, you can help—but remember to put these skills on your list so that others will know about them.

You can also express your skills as process, a description of how you work best. For example, you may have worked in many organizations and found that you are better working with people than with information, that your strengths are in speaking, supervising, teaching, negotiating, rather than in analyzing, computing, compiling, or synthesizing data. The annually revised manual *What Color Is Your Parachute?* by Richard Bolles is a helpful guide to thinking this way about your skills.

However you present it, this list is simply revealing what exists. As Michelangelo said about sculpture, "The idea is already there. All you have to do is remove the excess stone."

Time may seem your most precious resource, even though, as Bertrand Russell said, "to realize the unimportance of time is the gate to wisdom." A national survey recently cited lack of time as the number one reason people didn't do more volunteer work. But, as we know, time is relative, and it has a way of expanding when we find something we love to do.

If you are thinking about committing some time to compassionate social action, you may already have been reflecting on whether your current use of time reflects your priorities. If it doesn't, you can make some changes. It is important to think carefully about how much time you can give. If you try to give too much, you will put stress on the rest of your life, and you may stop helping altogether. Still, as Shoshana Pakciarz of Project Bread, the umbrella program for Boston's many soup kitchens, food pantries, and shelter feeding programs, says, "The more time a person gives to a project, the more meaningful it becomes. If a person gives a day a year to the Walk for Hunger or an hour a week working in a soup kitchen, it will help, but it is not until you begin to get more deeply involved that you begin to understand more and make more meaningful relationships. You get back what you put in." And although the value of a caring act by one person for another can never be measured in time, and change can happen in an instant when the veils of illusion disappear, we do give that more of a chance to happen when we give it more time. But you may also want to start by giving an amount of time that is easy for you, then let the work call you in; after a while, you may give more time because you want to, not because you think you ought to.

Many of us would like to give all or most of our time to working for change in the world or simply to taking care of our aging parents. Some of us can, either because we can live without a salary or because we have one of the too few paying jobs that are devoted to this work. Often, however, money presents itself as an obstacle as we try to commit more of our time to compassionate action. We don't have time because we have to work full-time just to support ourselves and our families or the community job pays too little to live on.

This is not likely to change. While it handsomely rewards those who work within its system, such as employees of the International Monetary Fund and the United Nations, society rarely rewards those who are trying to change it. And independent projects committed to improving the lives of the poor can rarely justify paying much of their income to the process. So we start by committing otherwise "free" time to this work or simplifying our lives so that we need less to live. Although living with less money than we are used to can often be difficult, living more simply does have the additional benefit of taking us closer to the concerns of people in deeper need, and it leads us to live in a style more appropriate for the earth. Living in smaller spaces with fewer cars and appliances, dressing more simply, turning off lights, and eating locally grown food—all of which can reduce expenses—are ways that we want to live anyhow now that we know more about the cost to the planet of more materialistic ways of life.

When money is more abundant, when it is a plentiful resource, then the challenge is to find ways to use it compassionately. In *Tales of the Hasidim,* there is a story about Rabbi Baruch, who talked about three ways of bringing money to the *zaddik,* the head of the temple: "Some say to themselves, 'I'll give him something. I am the kind of person who brings gifts to the zaddik.' Others think, 'If I give gifts to this devout man, it will profit me hereafter.' These want heaven to pay them interest. It is a loan. But there are some who know: 'God has put this money in my hand for the zaddik, and I am his messenger.' These serve with a full and open heart."

To be conscious philanthropists, we need to be messengers. In fact, the same basic guidelines apply to giving money as to other action. It may appear to be easier to write checks to Greenpeace than to crew on their ships, but at heart the two acts are the same. We need to find out what we are funding and make sure that it is in harmony with our principles. And we need to avoid creating more separation by stressing the roles of "giver" and "receiver": we need to shift our thinking so that we focus on who we are, and who we are becoming, rather than on what we have or don't have. This will bring us all closer together and remind us of our common humanity.

Among our other resources are the people in our lives—friends, family, colleagues, the person sitting next to us on a plane. They are not resources in the opportunistic sense that some eighties networking promoted, in which people saw others as objects, valuable only for what they could do for them. This is a process of cooperation, of finding people who have ideas, connections, skills, information, and encouragement that they want to share because it will help relieve suffering. One of the best ways to start looking for opportunities is to ask people you know: one friend may turn out to have a former lover on the board of a local hospice; another may be volunteering with Amnesty International. Start talking to people about what you want to do.

Sometimes friends are helpful simply by encouraging us to get started. Edie Jones, a project coordinator for the Boston Junior League, in which she supports programs working with teen mothers, said, "I got started through the people in my life. My mother always wanted me to do service, but it wasn't till I had some long talks with my best buddy, and she said, 'Do it!' That's how I got involved." Mimi Fariña, founder of Bread and Roses, which provides professional entertainment for hospitals and prisons, talks about how her friends helped her. "Lack of education, of college education, made me feel pretty inferior and insecure. So I did need to make those phone calls to people to say, 'Hey, I have this idea, and I don't know what to do with it. Where do I take it from here?' I did need to rely on my friends."

Finally, after you have searched your mind and heart for a comprehensive list of your resources, and it still looks a little thin or those resources you do have look inappropriate for the task at hand, remember that we are always in process, and new skills can always be learned. Bill Berkowitz, in a book about service called *Local Heroes,* says not to worry at all about resources at the beginning: "As a rule, the 'local hero' has no dollar subsidies, no specialized skills, no outside support at the onset. The slate may not be completely clean, but most resources are created and developed along the way."

So just look carefully and be honest about who you are and what you have to offer, let others know, and be open to learning more. At the very least, you will have created an interesting picture of yourself that will make it easier to express yourself to others and point you a little more clearly toward what comes next.

Enter Lightly

Flow with whatever may happen and let your mind be free. Stay centered by accepting whatever you are doing. This is the ultimate.

CHUANG TSU

If we are to help heal the world, we need to remember that it is a sacred place. Our actions need to be positive statements, reminders that even in the worst of times there is a world worth struggling for. We need to find ways to keep the vision alive, to acknowledge but not get caught in the dark side, to remember that even the worst aspects of suffering are only part of the whole picture. We need to enter lightly.

Entering lightly means not ignoring suffering but treating it gently. We don't want to ignore another's pain, but our becoming depressed or angry about it doesn't relieve it and may increase it. The delicate balance is in allowing ourselves to feel the pain fully, to be sad or angry or hurt by it, but not be so weighted down by it that we are unable to act to relieve it. It is a matter of ends and means again: to create a caring, loving, peaceful world, we need to act with care and love and peace.

Easy to say, you may think, remembering your heavy heart, tears, and anger when you first saw babies in Ethiopian refugee camps dying from malnutrition. But it is exactly at these times—in the presence of pain, injustice, and horror—that our equilibrium is most needed. How can we keep it? Meditation can help; singing or walking can help; talking with people we respect can help; simply being quiet with ourselves can help.

It is the continuing work of life: of learning to trust that the universe is unfolding exactly as it should, no matter how it looks to us; learning to appreciate that each of us has a part in nurturing this interconnected whole and healing it where it is torn; discovering what our individual contribution can be, then giving ourselves fully to it. Demanding as that sounds, it is what, in the spiritual sense, we are all here for, and compassionate action gives us yet one more opportunity to live it. It is an opportunity to cooperate with the universe, to be part of what the Chinese call the great river of the Tao. It is not a coincidence that Hanuman, who in the Hindu cosmology is called the "embodiment of selfless service," is the son of the wind god; when we give ourselves into becoming fully who we are by doing fully what we do, we experience lightness, we are like kites in wind, we are on the side of the angels, we are entering lightly.

Looking for lightness, we find there is one thing that can sometimes spring us out of the heavy places. What is this magic? In Woody Allen's *Stardust Memories,* the aliens, after looking around at life on earth, say, "You want to do mankind a real service? Tell funnier jokes." Laughter is healing, we all know that. It's very difficult to laugh and be angry at the same time. Laughter gives present reality a break.

Most people working with the more difficult realms of human existence know the value of humor in returning us to the incredible lightness of being. Lily Tomlin's bag lady Trudy, funky vehicle for truth in *The Search for Intelligent Life in the Universe*, helps us beyond the pity and superiority that we sometimes feel when we see an apparently crazy woman on the street. Trudy reflects to herself and the audience:

> See, the human mind is kind of like . . . a piñata. When it breaks open, there's a lot of surprises inside. Once you get the piñata perspective, you see that losing your mind can be a peak experience. I was not always a bag lady, you know, I used to be a designer and creative consultant. For big companies! Who do you think thought up the color scheme for Howard Johnson's? At the time, nobody was using orange and aqua in the same room together. With fried clams.

Trudy is lovable and brilliant in her madness. We realize that we were caught in our oh-poor-bag-ladies track—we haven't allowed for this possibility of brilliance. We have forgotten that it is all relative. We have gotten stuck thinking something very limited about who was inside that woman on the street who looked like Trudy. How different it all is from another perspective. That's part of what's funny. Not just how different it all looks but how limited our view is. Humor opens up reality. We remember that we don't always know the whole picture. And that's very liberating and lightening—there isn't only one way to see it all. What a relief!

Word leaked out of Israel that there were some very funny jokes made by some very funny Israeli comedians about how people looked in those gas masks when Tel Aviv was being bombed by Iraq. It didn't make the threat any less terrible, but, for a moment, people weren't stuck in a reality circumscribed by fear. They had become preposterous animals or extraterrestrials.

In 1990, a year that gave us the savings and loan scandal, Desert Shield, and cutbacks in nearly every social service, Wavy Gravy, court jester of the Hog Farm Commune, ran for city council in Berkeley with the slogan "Why not elect a real clown for a change?" He was not completely without a political portfolio: as he says, "I had run a pig—Pigasus—for president in 1968. In 1972, we ran a rock for that high office, with a roll for vice president. Then along came Nobody, and Nobody is still the perfect presidential candidate. Nobody cares about the poor. Nobody cares about the environment. Nobody represents us in Washington. Nobody makes apple pie like Mom. From 1976 to the present, I've worked for Nobody, cuz Nobody is in Washington working for me!" But this time, at the local level, Wavy was running himself. Promoted by flamingo lawn signs designed by R. We Really, Wavy promised more creeks and fewer cars, campgrounds for the homeless, and whistle rings and hooter horns at the weekly council meetings. Wavy said about the council, "They tend to get lost in their own Berkeleyness. I think I can lighten things up." Even with his pledge to put a chicken in every pothole, Wavy lost the election, but he won 2,000 of the 6,000 votes, partly because people felt that a little humor is what politics really needs. Humor, Wavy says, helps life go more smoothly; it's the rubber between the elevator doors. "And don't forget," he adds, "if you don't have a sense of humor, it just isn't funny."

It is not always easy to be light in the presence of pain and suffering and politics, but remember that, when we are not, it is a signal to be careful. We may be clinging to an idea of how things should be rather than simply looking at how they are. We may have forgotten that all of us have something important to give, but it is different for each one of us. There was once a hungry pig and chicken walking toward a diner with a neon sign saying BACON AND EGGS. The chicken hurried toward it, but the pig hestitated. "For you," he said to the chicken, "it's a contribution; for me it's a commitment."

We need to catch ourselves and laugh. When we find ourselves on the way to an interview at Greenpeace to see how we can help the environment, and we notice that we are drinking Folger's (boycotted) coffee from a (Styrofoam) cup, we can resolve to change our ways, but first we deserve a good laugh. We're doing the best we can, and if we appreciate ourselves and others along the way, if we stay light, we'll be able to do a lot more.

Opportunities for Action

You say nothing is created new?
Don't worry about it. With the mud of the earth,
make a cup from which your brother can drink.

ANTONIO MACHADO

The next time you are in a science museum, visit the hologram exhibit. On a two-dimensional surface, you will see three-dimensional images, often of the eye or of a family sitting around a dining-room table. Such a three-dimensional image is remarkable itself, especially to people who were alive before television, but the more remarkable aspect of holograms is that you can cut them in pieces and look again, and each piece will still contain the whole image. This scientific demonstration makes graphic to even the most pragmatic among us what was always known to mystics: the whole is contained in each of its parts, the macrocosm exists within the microcosm. There are ways in which this is also true of suffering. Since we are all part of a common reality, all suffering is contained in each small experience of suffering. The suffering of each of us—every whale and every distant hungry child—affects us all, and none of us will be truly free until we all are.

So if you choose to defend the rain forest, you will also be working for better health for inner-city kids. Relieving suffering anywhere, or helping to create an environment in which suffering is more likely to be relieved, shifts the balance slightly and affects everything else. In this case, the very air that everyone—inner-city kids included—breathes improves, so health improves. But, also, consciousness changes; the people involved, including us, get closer to an understanding of living right on the planet, which changes political and economic and social behavior, which then affects others in increasing circles like those from a pebble dropped in water. So, although it is good to find a right match for who we are and what we have to offer, it also doesn't matter where we start; it is all interconnected.

Look around. The world is now offering us extraordinary opportunities to serve. After even the briefest investigation, any of us will find many things we can do to decrease suffering, to empower others to take better care of their lives, and, as geotheologian Thomas Berry says, "to learn to live graciously together on this unique, beautiful, blue planet." This time of looking for an opportunity, of not knowing where we want to start, encourages us to have what the great Zen teacher Shunryu Suzuki-Roshi called "beginner's mind." In the beginner's mind, he would say, there are many possibilities. In the expert's mind there are few. When we are looking for a way to practice compassionate action, opportunities abound; when we consider them with beginner's mind, we are more likely to find some that are a good match for just who we are.

This chapter contains some suggestions for ways to serve. Some are rather conventional; others are from less frequently followed paths. They are offered not only as specific suggestions but also as stimulants for the imagination, reminders that there are many ways in each of our communities that will allow us to act with fresh ideas and vision and care and love.

WORKING WITH AIDS: CONFRONTING DEATH AND NURTURING LIFE

"I went to a meeting with about fifteen people when it was first beginning to happen, before it was called AIDS, in the fall of 1982. Each person in the circle said what they thought would be needed, and I just said 'hospice.' I thought that people were going to be isolated in their dying, especially isolated because this disease was looking so weird and so scary. I knew that these people were going to be pushed to the periphery and that they were going to be frightened, and they were going to need someone to be there.

"And I was the only person who said that—hospice—so everyone said, 'Okay, you do that.' My first surprise was that I was the only one who said it, and my second was that they thought I had the potential to do it. That activated me, I felt charged with it, and I gathered people who felt the same way. We took some hospice training, and so it began." This is the voice of Peter

Lombardi, former volunteer coordinator at the hospice at Mission Hill, Boston.

In many of our communities, acquired immunodeficiency syndrome (AIDS), a consequence of human immunodeficiency virus (HIV), has brought us face to face with fear and discrimination and death, our own as well as others'. The statistics alone are staggering: there are as many as 8 to 10 million people infected with HIV worldwide, and the World Health Organization estimates that 1 million people will have developed AIDS by 1991. In New York City, AIDS is now one of the leading causes of death for women of childbearing age; 1 out of every 61 babies there is HIV-infected. Although AIDS first affected gay men most significantly, people of color, for whom services, education, health care, and drug treatment are less available, are now at far greater risk.

Obviously, an immense, internationally organized public health response to the epidemic is needed. The major work of research, education, and treatment has to be handled by governments and institutions. But even if they were responding effectively, there would still be many things each of us could do to help. Loving-kindness and honest acceptance are in short supply.

If you are drawn to help and don't know where to start, call the AIDS action group in your community (AIDS is in the phone book at the beginning of the A listings, with the acronyms). They will help you discover the many needs in the AIDS community. You may also have friends in the gay or inner-city communities who know of opportunities or other friends who are nurses, doctors, therapists, or counselors; many of our lives are now touched by AIDS.

There are some actions we can all take, such as becoming better educated about AIDS, learning how it is transmitted and how it is not. As the San Francisco AIDS Foundation says, "The best defense against AIDS is information." We can share accurate information with family, friends, and community—even information that did not used to be considered appropriate to share. Parents especially can talk with their children and encourage the schools to do so.

We can all examine our fears about AIDS and how those fears are keeping us from helping. Fear permeates the AIDS environment. James Curran, director of the Division of HIV/AIDS at the Centers for Disease Control, speaks of the very estimates of the numbers of people infected with the HIV virus as "very frightening." The life-styles of the groups most at risk in North America— gay men, intravenous drug users, the poor—are frightening to many others. Patients have begun to be afraid of their doctors and dentists; policemen are afraid of bleeding victims. The entire epidemic, so often in the news, so often affecting people we know or at least hear about, puts us in touch with our fear of death, our fear of the unknown. In a culture where we have tried to mask and ignore death, to keep it invisible inside rosewood coffins, AIDS is disquieting at a profound level.

The good news is that there is something for us all to do. We can all examine our fears and prejudices. We can meet with others and talk about what is disturbing to us, and how we can support positive efforts for treatment, research, care, and, most fundamentally, the attitudes that form the psychological climate. We can explore how fear can lead toward panic, toward the restrictions of individual rights in the name of safety. We can explore the issues of community responsibility at a time of such a health threat. We can share our own fears—for ourselves, our friends, and our children and ask for help in working through them. We can give condoms for Valentine's Day to break taboos. We can recognize this epidemic as an opportunity to open our hearts to one another and recognize our common humanity.

We can all write to our legislators. Connecticut Governor and former Senator Lowell Weicker, an outspoken advocate for AIDS research and education, says, "You don't need to be a highly paid, professional lobbyist to make a mark on AIDS spending or policy. Every constituent call is listened to. Every letter is read. Even if they do not change the officeholder's mind or vote, they send a crucial message that somebody cares and so should they. A constituent's firsthand experience with the disease can help bridge the gap between AIDS in the abstract and AIDS as an everyday matter of life and death." Once you become educated about the current AIDS crisis, you may want to write to encourage funding for AIDS education or research, here and in other countries; you may encourage a national health care system that will guarantee coverage to AIDS patients; you may focus on laws to protect people who are HIV positive from discrimination in employment, housing, education, and health care. The more you learn and the more you are able to keep your heart open to this suffering, the more articulate you will become about your concerns.

There are many practical needs in the AIDS community that any of us can take care of, either alone or by forming a direct action group. A group of friends in

Cambridge painted a government shelter for persons with AIDS. Others have started housework groups, food banks, or clothing exchanges. Frequently people with AIDS need people to pick up medicine, fix a meal, or call and say they care. They need to hear positive news, be supported in their decisions, and be reminded that they are still valued.

A unique role that has emerged from the special needs of people with AIDS is the buddy, a kind of committed friend or helpmate who volunteers time and understanding. There are now programs that prepare and continue to support people who choose this role, since being a committed friend to a person who is dying can make deep demands and can lead us to confront our own mortality. Peter Lombardi, who started the buddy program in Boston, describes the training as a kind of self-examination in which one asks questions such as, "Who am I right now at this point in my life?" "Why am I here, asking to be part of the buddy program?" "What do I need from this?" Being a buddy can be as simple as making weekly phone calls or visits or providing a ride to the doctor; it can mean grocery shopping, errand running, or light housecleaning. But it can also call forth deep emotion and involvement. Listen to Francis Giambrone speaking about a man to whom he was a buddy: "He would ask questions and he would force me to think about things I hadn't thought about. He knew he was dying, he admitted it. When he was scared about it, he could talk about it. It was profound. . . . I knew I was crossing a line, and I knew I would pay for it . . . and I did. He took me to a lot of scary places . . . and he opened up my faith again."

There are other ways as well to make a difference concerning AIDS. Organizations such as ACT UP (AIDS Coalition to Unleash Power) provide opportunities for public action to dramatize the need for change; "die-ins" to publicize the lack of government spending on AIDS are one example. ACT NOW (AIDS Coalition to Network, Organize, and Win) and other organizations publish information and provide networking for individuals and groups working on different aspects of the problem. Such organizations often need volunteer help.

You can still stitch a memorial panel and make a donation to the NAMES Project, which is constructing the growing patchwork quilt that honors and celebrates and remembers many of those who have died from AIDS. In the arts, many extraordinary performances have evoked the emotions brought forth by the disease while sharing helpful information. Funds are always needed by existing AIDS groups, and you can raise them in an endless number of ways, which have already included elegant meals by local chefs, art auctions, theatrical performances, raffles, runs, and a concert by the Grateful Dead and Los Lobos. Try one of these fund-raisers, or allow something entirely new to come forth. Only you know what you can do best to help. As you go, you may be inspired by these words of Rainer Maria Rilke:

> . . . that one can contain
> death, the whole of death . . .
> can hold it to one's heart
> gently, and not refuse to go on living,
> is inexpressible.

BEING A CITIZEN DIPLOMAT

"The basic problem is not political, it is apolitical and human. One of the most important things to do is to keep cutting deliberately through political lines and barriers and emphasizing that these are largely fabrications and that there is a genuine reality: the human dimension." These are the words of the Christian mystic Thomas Merton; their spirit has influenced many American citizens, who believe that if we know one another better we are less likely to create war and suffering.

In 1987, for example, 120,000 Americans visited the USSR, many of them believing that genuine person-to-person contact would begin to heal divisions between the countries at a time when official diplomacy seemed hopelessly unproductive. Many high school classes traded students for a week or two, during which not a few seventeen-year-olds discovered cross-cultural romance. Groups of doctors studied one another's techniques for surgery. Counselors of alcoholics came to the United States to study twelve-step programs, and rock musicians played in Moscow what the Soviet press called "proletarian rage against the excesses of the first world." Joseph Goldstein and Sharon Salzberg, teachers at the Insight Meditation Society in Barre, Massachusetts, taught insight meditation in Leningrad. And some people went on their own simply to meet the Soviets and help dissolve the preconceptions that all separated people hold, especially those who have been educated with myths of enemies as the "evil empire." These were seeds planted that now—in a new era for the Soviets—can flower.

One North American traveler told of getting off a bus in Zagreb, Yugoslavia, on her way east. It was the first Eastern European country she had visited. Although at the time she considered herself politically a progressive, as the bus drove into the city in the late afternoon, the sky was gray, the shop windows were almost empty, and people walked through the streets in heavy, dark over- coats, hunched against the cold. The images were so true to what she had learned growing up in the cold war fifties that all the connotations of *Communist* she had been taught in her Catholic grammar school came flooding back. She remembered crouching under her desk to protect herself against an atomic bomb and praying for the poor lost souls, "Savior of the World, save Russia." As she stepped off the bus and toward a stand selling hot cheese pastries, she saw a man walking toward her, a Communist, the Ultimate Other, the enemy. He looked directly at her, right into her American eyes, and said in heavily accented English, "I love you." There was no more enemy.

When asked to work for nuclear disarmament, social activist Fran Peavey was confronted with this same sense of separation from others. "I thought, 'How can I possi- bly work against nuclear weapons from an American bias when nuclear weapons is the whole world. I've only or- ganized locally in San Francisco, and mostly I only *love* people in San Francisco and Idaho. I don't love people in the rest of the world.' I had never thought of myself as being very interested in travel—I thought people who traveled were unhappy. But now I had a reason to travel because I needed to have people in my heart whom I loved, in order to work against nuclear weapons. And so I got one of the scariest ideas I'd ever had. I sold my house and bought a smaller house and with some of that money I bought a round-the-world ticket, and I started off. I told everybody I was doing that, but I didn't tell them what I really needed to do, because I didn't know whether it was a good thing to do: I sat in parks in cities where I didn't know anybody and I held a sign saying AMERICAN WILLING TO LISTEN. And I met people, and we talked together, and by the time I came home there were people I cared about in many places in the world and I could work against nuclear weapons. It's not really enough to love people different from oneself; it's important to work for our common interest. But I still didn't know whether I had done a good thing—it seemed like such a strange thing to have to do—until I told other people and they all thought it had been a very good thing."

If you are not drawn to travel alone to break down barriers, you can also be a citizen diplomat as part of a group, often combining some kind of service work with travel. During the eighties, many people traveled to Nicaragua to help with coffee harvests, give technical support for water and electricity projects, supply tools and spare parts unavailable during the U.S. embargo, teach in the countrywide literacy program, help build the public health system, and learn about the life of the Nicaraguan people. Although in many Third World situations the aim of awakened development projects is to empower local people and not to continue dependence on First World expatriates, there are certain circumstances in which hands-on help is appropriate: in these situations, the understanding, the long-term friendships, and the spirit of solidarity that result are often as important as the immediate aid. In the case of Nicaragua, the local people came to understand that all Americans did not support the official U.S. position against their country, and a network of support and care began to grow that led North Americans to question U.S. policies such as support for the Contras.

Churches, universities, unions, and community groups, as well as organizations developed specifically for solidarity with other regions, often offer opportunities for these people-to-people connections. Sister city or sister parish links are common these days; if one doesn't exist in your community, it's possible to start one. Cambridge, Massachusetts, has a sister city in El Salvador. Groups of citizens visit twice a year, taking with them some financial help raised through local telethons, dinners, and other functions, personalized gifts from children and others, and their care and support and encouragement for this group of people living through very difficult times. When their Salvadoran sister town was threatened by the military, the people of Cambridge initiated a successful rapid response campaign, in which residents called and wrote congresspeople in the United States and then President Cristiani in El Salvador to stop the harassment.

There are many issues to consider before setting off as a citizen diplomat—which kind of organization to connect with, the delicate balance between aid and development, the kind of aid that is appropriate, problems of visiting countries with repressive governments, the establishment of true dialogue, and so on. But if this way of working for peace through friendship draws you, there are people and resources that can help you ask the right questions. We have listed some of them in the directory at the end of this book.

WORKING FOR PEACE

Lord, make me an instrument of thy peace.
Where there is hatred, let me sow love.
Where there is injury, pardon.
Where there is doubt, faith.
Where there is despair, hope.
Where there is darkness, light,
and where there is sadness, joy.
May I never seek so much to be consoled as to console,
To be understood as to understand,
To be loved as to love.
For it is in pardoning that we are forgiven,
It is in giving that we receive,
It is in dying that we are born to eternal life.

ST. FRANCIS OF ASSISI

Everybody wants peace. General Norman Schwarzkopf kept the Prayer of St. Francis next to his pillow during the Gulf War, in which reports say that over 100,000 people died. Those who led us into that war, and those who supported it, often with great reluctance, all said they wanted peace but felt that war was their only alternative. Since that war, many of us who believe that the way to peace is not through violence are realizing that long-lasting peace will require not only last-minute demonstrations at air force bases, well-meaning as those may be, but, as Albert Einstein said, a whole new way of thinking, a whole new set of alternatives. For the future we need to find ways to avoid situations in which massive killing appears as the only choice. We need to recognize that war does not begin the moment it is "declared" but is the logical culmination of a set of values and understandings that lead us, inexorably, toward only certain possible responses to a challenge.

If we are to have peaceful coexistence on the planet, we need to reeducate ourselves and share that understanding with others. We need to think about what it means to be part of a common humanity, in which none of us wants to lose our daughters, sons, mothers, or fathers to war or our children to hunger. Then, recognizing that conflict arises even in the most loving families, we need to learn new ways of resolving it: ways that are respectful of and satisfying to everyone involved, that open the path for growth in the future, that respect healthy balances of local self-reliance and international interdependence. As Alexander Pope said over two hundred years ago, "Conflict should always be managed as to remember that the only true end of it is peace."

This is not a simple task. Meg Gage, executive director of the Peace Development Fund, says, "War doesn't come just because we have weapons; it's a whole chain of attitudes, thoughts, and behaviors that leads us there. And all the work to change these is important. It's not enough to think that if I lead a kind, friendly, and peaceful life, and become a vegetarian, that the world will be peaceful. That's not enough. And getting rid of weapons isn't enough. We got rid of the B-1 bomber, and we got the B-2. The challenge is to do all these things at once: work for the elimination of weapons, talk about foreign policy, look at how we see other people in the world as our minions, look at racism and violence in our own lives and in our society, learn and teach nonviolent conflict resolution. There are many parts to this, and whichever one we choose, it helps all the others. We have to get over feeling ridiculous, impotent, about working for peace. It's true that there *is* power in the individual humble act. Most of the world is walking down the road in the wrong direction; individual acts won't stop that, but they can help to slow it down. As Gandhi said, 'Your act may be very small, it may seem insignificant, but it's very important that you do it.' We can each start walking in the other direction."

How can you start working for peace? You can work in the schools; every community has them. Set up a conflict resolution program, or support the one that already exists. There are models, materials, and people to help you do this. The National Association for Mediation in Education (NAME) has a directory of all the conflict resolution programs in the country and can help you get started.

You can work for change through your congresspeople. Build a group to affect their thinking and leadership as well as their votes. 20/20 Vision is a nationwide network to help people do just that. Each month, project leaders select an action that local citizens can do in twenty minutes; as one of the 20/20 brochures says, it's a program that allows you to defuse nuclear bombs on your coffee break. Each month members receive a card with brief background information and a suggested twenty-minute action, such as calling a congressperson to ask her or him to be present for certain votes and to vote for certain amendments.

You can create study circles or "salons." Many of us aren't involved in particular issues not because we don't care but because we can't figure them out. Meeting in groups to find out more about any issue, from politics in the Middle East to the curriculum in your local school, can be informative and build community. Often action for change emerges spontaneously when people begin to feel they know the basics. The Movement for a New Society supplies information and models for taking a group from small to large circles of thought and ending with an action.

You can focus on the military presence in your own community. Find out whether weapons or parts of weapons are manufactured there, and, with enough citizens to form a critical mass, encourage those companies to build something other than a bomb in your backyard. Find out what research is being conducted at nearby universities; let them know that you don't want those microbes escaping from their lab. Do an environmental impact study and publicize the danger of toxic waste from weapons. Find out what is being transported through your community or dumped there, and publicize it. Concerned Citizens for Nuclear Safety in New Mexico, when they learned that the federal government planned to make New Mexico the first underground repository for nuclear wastes generated by the weapons industry, published *Radiation Rag*: "All the news that's hot to trot, brought to you for 240,000 years."

Boycott weapons manufacturers. You probably weren't going to buy weapons anyway, but many of these companies, such as General Electric, manufacture domestic products as well. *Shopping for a Better World* and *Rating America's Corporate Conscience* are two guides that will help you find out who makes what. INFACT reports that their three-year-old boycott against GE decreased revenues from individual consumers by at least $55 million, increased advertising costs, and made it harder to recruit employees. Intensive efforts of activists in Nevada, northern California, and Hawaii convinced Safeway to provide alternatives to GE light bulbs in 300 of their stores nationwide. If you want to know about existing boycotts, subscribe to *Boycott Action News,* published by Co-op America.

Finally, our lives can be statements of peace. We can learn to live more lovingly, to resolve conflicts without aggression. We can look at racism in our lives and find ways to end it. We can reduce our consumption of mass consumer items that foster dependence on Third World resources. "No blood for oil" would be a stronger argument if we were using less oil. We can recycle, drive less, eat locally produced organic food, plant trees, and begin to live in a way that respects the needs of others. These can be the first steps of many toward peace.

Take the Leap

Whatever you can do or dream you can do, begin it.
Boldness has genius, power, and magic to it.

JOHANN WOLFGANG VON GOETHE

The journey of a thousand miles begins with a single step, and we all know that the first step can be the hardest. Joe Gorin, executive director of the Network in Solidarity with the People of Guatemala, said this of his start with Central America: "In 1980, a close North American friend of mine was killed in Guatemala, and I began to feel called to go there. I knew the suffering there was great and the awareness of it here was low. But I was getting my doctorate in psychology, and I didn't have time for social action. Then I began to have this intensive urge to learn Spanish—I listened to tapes in the car and taught myself. But it wasn't until 1987—seven years later—that I finally went."

Whether it's calling Oxfam America to see if they need our help or setting out those four brown bags to recycle the household trash, we've all had trouble with beginnings. Musicians say that the hardest part of practicing is taking the instrument out of the case. But as Jonathan Schell said when reflecting on how we could build a livable world now that we have nuclear weapons: "Every person is the right person to act. Every moment is the right moment to begin." Take out that saxophone. Get the process going. Be bold. Take the first step. Make the leap. Act from your wild dream of a more loving, more just world.

Of course it is useful to be reflective at the beginning, to learn what we can about the situation at hand and to have a good sense of our own motivations, skills, talents, and passions, so that the first step is at least pointed in the right direction. But once we have a good sense of these things, too much rumination can keep us from getting into the process, which is where we will really learn. We do not want to take on more than we can do with clarity of mind and an open heart, but once we begin to awaken to the suffering of others and the interconnection that binds us, we know we have to do what we can to aid those who are hurting. Our understanding of the interlocking nature of all beings is not a subject for intellectual analysis; it is an imperative for action.

Many beginnings are scary, and we are afraid to take the first step. Think of all the frightening beginnings you have known: going to school on the first day, meeting your new stepfather, skiing downhill, eating tofu, stepping off a bus in Zagreb, making love, giving birth, getting divorced—whatever it has been for each of us, we all know those moments of hesitation that come from fear at the beginning. It is, of course, fear of the unknown, of how we will be changed in unidentifiable ways. A friend who was drawn to learn aikido went to watch a demonstration class at Kenai Sensei's dojo in Cambridge. When the class was over, she walked through the city, feeling a single emotion in her whole body and mind. At first she couldn't identify what it was; then she realized it was fear. Oh, she thought, I must be afraid that I can't do it—that I won't be able to do a forward roll, that I'll be thrown too hard and break a bone, that I'll fail. But that didn't feel like the truth, and she began to realize that what she was afraid of was that she *would* be able to do it, that it would become a passion, and it would change her in ways that she couldn't predict or understand. Once she recognized that terror for what it was, she turned around, went back to the dojo, and signed up.

Compassionate action does change us, and if you sense that at the beginning, you are right. Anything that we approach as a "path," or a way of learning or opening, has power, and it can be frightening. But it also has attraction because the deeper part of ourselves wants to change, to open, to free ourselves from fear. So we embrace the opportunity. We step onto the mat.

A student in a New York Open Center course on compassion in action said that she was afraid of homeless people. "I guess because I have and they don't. I had been giving them some clothes at night when I wouldn't actually have to meet people, because I've been really afraid. And then this time I brought the coats during a mealtime and I said, 'If you guys could use these . . .' I was shaking, I was so scared. And they were so gracious."

Working with the homeless, the poor, and others at the edge reminds us of our own vulnerability and the compromises we may have made in our lives to create material security. Working with AIDS or other terminally ill patients is frightening because it often reveals our fear of our own death. Working with international issues shows us the fragile balances in the world order and how close we always are to war and the abuse of nuclear power. Working with the environment reveals deep fears of losing the very ground beneath our feet and the air we breathe. But these fears are there, within us, anyhow. When they become more apparent, it is a gift. We can see them and work with them. In aikido and other martial arts, fear is considered a friend. It keeps you awake to what is there. If you are afraid, your mind will not stray, you will not fall asleep. When you want to improve a certain move, you choose a fiercer partner to keep your mind completely centered on the action. Although true freedom is an open state of fearlessness, while we are still afraid we can use fear to increase our awareness.

If raw fear is not holding us back, sometimes our need for control keeps us from acting. We hesitate to take the first step because we don't know what the second, third, or fourth step will be. We feel that we need a perfect or at least a very well developed plan before we can go forward. On the contrary, such a plan is impossible to make—it is acting itself that teaches us how to act. As the situation changes, and we stay awake and aware, new possibilities for action reveal themselves. Flexibility, curiosity, and willingness to listen and learn are what we need for success in this work. It is often necessary to go forward *not* knowing what will happen, willing to let the way take shape. As Neem Karoli Baba once said, "You can plan for five hundred years, but you don't know what will happen in the next moment."

Of course, it is useful to set goals, as farmers do when they plant their corn and plan their harvests, but it is not until we get into the work that we find out about the richness of the soil, the amount of rainfall, the pests and plagues, and the styles and habits of the other farmers with whom we are working. From these factors, we learn gradually and idiosyncratically, and we adapt and readapt our ways. In *Pedagogy of the Oppressed,* his landmark work on literacy and the poor, Brazilian educator Paulo Freire said truth is revealed though a "dialogue with the world," which includes soil, rain, and farmers. We need to begin the work in order to start experiencing reality as process, as transformation, rather than as a static entity. Spiritual teacher J. Krishnamurti said, "An ideal actually prevents direct action upon what is. To have peace, we will have to begin not to live an ideal life but to see things as they are and transform them." We need to accept our plans as works in progress, commit ourselves to the task at hand, be open to change, give up our attachment to a certain set of results, and get started!

In the great Hindu myth the *Ramayana,* Hanuman was challenged to serve: Prince Rama asked him to leap across the ocean between India and Sri Lanka, carrying Rama's gold ring and a message of love to the princess Sita, who was being held hostage by the evil, ten-headed Ravana. Hanuman, the "little monkey," was not sure that he would be able to do it, and he had no idea what might await him on the other shore. He hesitated, thinking that maybe someone else would be better for the job. But, as the story goes, "there was dismay and faint sorrow, and it was time to be strong." So Hanuman agreed to take the ring to Sita. He climbed to a high hilltop overlooking the vast ocean separating the two countries, and then, in the translation of William Buck,

> he held his breath and sucked in his stomach. He frisked his tail and raised it a little on the end. He bent his knees and swung back his arms, and on one finger gleamed Rama's gold ring. Then, without pausing to think, he drew in his neck, laid back his ears, and jumped.
>
> It was grand! It was the greatest leap ever taken. The speed of Hanuman's jump pulled blossoms and flowers into the air after him, and they fell like little stars on the waving treetops. The animals on the beach had never seen such a thing. They cheered Hanuman, then the air burned from his passage, and red clouds flamed over the sky, and Hanuman was far out of sight of land.

LIGHT ON THE PATH

Mirabai Bush

Words from the Heart:
A Bibliography on Compassion

THE BASICS

Where the meaning of compassion was first expressed:

> The Bible
> The Koran
> The Dhammapada
> The Bhagavad Gita
> The Ramayana
> The Tao Te Ching
> The Popul Vuh

WORDS OF INSPIRATION

Annis, Sheldon, and Hakim, Peter, eds. *Direct to the Poor: Grass-roots Development in Latin America.* Rienner, 1988.

An exploration of the idea of poor people creating and controlling their own institutions and lives. This is a book about small victories.

Berry, Thomas. *The Dream of the Earth.* Sierra Club, 1990.

The sweetest, finest articulation of the interconnected nature of the spirit and the earth.

Berry, Wendell. *What Are People For?* esp. "Healing." North Point, 1990.

Poems and essays that return us to the basics of relationship.

Blofeld, John. *Bodhisattva of Compassion: The Mystical Tradition of Kuan Yin.* Shambhala, 1988.

Stories of Tara, Avalokiteshvara, and Kuan Yin.

Dass, Ram, and Gorman, Paul. *How Can I Help?: Stories and Reflections on Service.* Alfred A. Knopf, 1985.

A practical helper's companion. Provides support and inspiration; includes many deeply moving stories of service. Norman Cousins called it "a colorful road map away from helplessness."

Davies, Peter, ed. *Human Rights.* Routledge Chapman and Hall, 1989.

Essays on women's rights, children's rights, apartheid, genocide, indigenous peoples, and so on to commemorate the fortieth anniversary of the U.N. Universal Declaration of Human Rights.

Elgin, Duane. *Voluntary Simplicity: Toward a Way of Life That Is Outwardly Simple, Inwardly Rich.* William Morrow, 1981.

The classic statement of how to live a life marked by frugal consumption, ecological awareness, and personal growth.

Eppsteiner, Fred, ed. *The Path of Compassion: Writings on Socially Engaged Buddhism.* Parallax, 1988.

Fine essays on the implications of "a deep sense of oneness with all beings, a spontaneous impulse born of suffering." Contributors include Joanna Macy, Gary Snyder, and Jack Kornfield.

Farren, Pat, ed. **A Way of Life: Celebrating Sustained Activism, 1991 Peace Calendar.** War Resisters League, 1991.

Technically a calendar, this wonderful collection includes the stories of many people who have been living long lives of service. Those who walked ahead.

Fox, Matthew. **A Spirituality Named Compassion, and the Healing of the Global Village, Humpty Dumpty, and Us.** Harper & Row, 1979.

An exploration of compassion in the context of creation spirituality.

Freire, Paulo. **Pedagogy of the Oppressed.** Continuum, 1986.

A passionate exploration of liberation, oppression, dialogue, cooperation, and mutual support. Freire, who introduced literacy programs to the slums of Brazil, discovered for himself the essential nature of the helping relationship.

Gandhi, Mahatma. **The Words of Gandhi,** selected by Richard Attenborough. Newmarket, 1982.

A slim volume of essence quotations. Good for travel and for gifts.

Giono, Jean. **The Man Who Planted Trees.** Chelsea Green, 1985. Also sold with a cassette of the story read by Robert J. Lurtsema, with original music by Paul Winter.

A wonderful story of someone who simply did it—and did it simply.

Gutiérrez, Gustavo. **The Power of the Poor in History: Selected Writings.** Orbis, 1983.

Pleas for "acts of faith, love, and hope in active participation to liberate persons from everything that dehumanizes them and prevents them from living according to the word of God." By the father of liberation theology.

Gyatso, Tenzin, the Fourteenth Dalai Lama. **Kindness, Clarity, and Insight.** Snow Lion, 1984.

Reflections on living a life of kindness toward ourselves and others.

Ingram, Catherine. **In the Footsteps of Gandhi: Conversations with Spiritual Social Activists.** Parallax, 1990.

Interviews about the teachings of Gandhi, including nonviolence, with Cesar Chavez, Joan Baez, Bishop Desmond Tutu, Ram Dass, and others.

King, Martin Luther, Jr. **The Trumpet of Conscience.** Harper & Row, 1989.

A collection that includes the "I Have a Dream" speech and others that still ring in our ears.

Kome, Penney, and Crean, Patrick, eds. **Peace: A Dream Unfolding.** Sierra Club, 1986.

A big book of inspirational quotations, pictures, and poems. A good reminder of how peace has concerned all kinds of people throughout time.

Kozol, Jonathan. **Rachel and Her Children: Homeless Families in America.** Crown, 1987.

Full of poignant details, the stories of women and their children in New York's welfare hotels.

Loeb, Paul. **Hope in Hard Times: America's Peace Movement and the Reagan Era.** Lexington, 1986.

A book about "ordinary heroes." Philip Berrigan called it "therapy for bewildered consciences, tired spirits, and jaded lives."

Macy, Joanna. **Dharma and Development: Religion as Resource in the Sarvodaya Self-help Movement,** rev. ed. Kumarian, 1985.

Insights from time spent with the Sarvodaya movement for village development in Sri Lanka.

Nhat Hanh, Thich. **Being Peace.** Parallax, 1987.
————. **Peace Is Every Step: The Path of Mindfulness in Everyday Life.** Bantam, 1991.

Lessons in peace. To create a happy and peaceful world, we must be happy and peaceful ourselves. When Vietnamese Buddhist teacher Thich Nhat Hanh tells us this, it is as if we have never before heard it.

Partnoy, Alicia, ed. **You Can't Drown the Fire: Latin American Women Writing in Exile.** Cleis, 1988.

Works by women who have faced exile, torture, and death. They will remind you that the spirit never dies.

Peavey, Fran. **A Shallow Pool of Time: An HIV + Woman Grapples with the AIDS Epidemic.** New Society, 1990.

The moving journal of awakening as a Bay Area activist and "atomic comic" discovers that she is HIV positive.

Schumacher, E. F. **Small Is Beautiful: Economics as if People Mattered.** Harper & Row, 1973.

A basic statement of working together sensibly for change. If you haven't read it for years, read it again.

Titmuss, Christopher. **Spirit for Change: Voices of Hope in a World in Crisis.** Green Print, 1989.

Interviews in the spirit of engaged Buddhism on inner awareness, attitudes toward creatures and planet, and the psychology of change.

Tulku, Tarthang. **Gesture of Balance: A Guide to Awareness, Self-healing, and Meditation.** Dharma, 1977.

Gentle guidance on compassion and opening the heart.

Williams, Juan. **Eyes on the Prize: America's Civil Rights Years, 1954–1965.** Penguin, 1987.

Great photos and inspiring words from the movement that awakened many of our hearts. You've seen the TV series; now read the book.

Woodhouse, Tom, ed. **People and Planet: Alternative Nobel Prize Speeches.** Green, 1987.

"Alternative" statements such as "When one has reached the edge of the abyss, the only thing that makes sense is to step back."

BIOGRAPHY/AUTOBIOGRAPHY

Branch, Taylor. **Parting the Waters: America in the King Years, 1954–63.** Simon & Schuster, 1988.

The whole passionate story, a reminder of the deep spirituality that infused Martin Luther King, Jr.'s activism.

Coles, Robert. **Dorothy Day: A Radical Devotion.** Addison-Wesley, 1987.

A loving portrait of the sophisticated Greenwich Village novelist and reporter who combined spirituality and radical politics to start the Catholic Worker "Hospitality Houses" for the lonely, troubled, and destitute.

Downey, Michael. *A Blessed Weakness: The Spirit of Jean Vanier and L'Arche.* Harper & Row, 1986.

The story of Jean Vanier, who invited mentally retarded adults to live with him in rural France at his small community called The Ark; now there are sixty affiliated l'Arche communities around the world. One chapter is called "The Heart Knows."

Gonzalez-Balado, José Luis, and Playfoot, Janet, eds. *My Life for the Poor: Mother Teresa of Calcutta.* Harper & Row, 1985.

Biography of a life committed to service and the spirit. "Love until it hurts."

Gyatso, Tenzin, the Fourteenth Dalai Lama. *Freedom in Exile: The Autobiography of the Dalai Lama.* HarperCollins, 1990.

The story of the Dalai Lama's life and retreat from Tibet and his resettlement in India, where he became an international ambassador of compassion.

Horton, Myles, and Kohl, Herbert. *The Long Haul: An Autobiography.* Doubleday, 1990.

Autobiography of the founder of Highlander Folk School in Tennessee, started to "provide opportunities for people to grow." Rosa Parks grew there, and Martin Luther King, Jr., Pete Seeger, Eleanor Roosevelt, and others. You can grow by reading this.

Mandela, Winnie. *A Part of My Soul Went with Him.* W. W. Norton, 1985.

Letters between Nelson and Winnie Mandela that give a glimmer of why his presence was so shining after twenty-eight years of prison, and just how hard it was for Winnie as a single parent in Soweto.

Menchu, Rigoberta. *I, Rigoberta Menchu: An Indian Woman in Guatemala.* Verso, 1985.

A poignant story of growing up Mayan in a Spanish culture.

Sheehy, Gail. *The Spirit of Survival.* William Morrow, 1986.

The account of how a middle-class New York City journalist goes to the Cambodian refugee camps, hears the story of the Pol Pot holocaust, adopts a young Cambodian girl, and watches her own life turn upside down.

Shoumatoff, Alex. *The World Is Burning: Murder in the Rain Forest (The Tragedy of Chico Mendes).* Little, Brown, 1990.

The complicated ramifications of rain forest burning woven into the story of environmentalist Chico Mendes, killed for organizing the rubber tappers of Acre in Brazil.

CALLS TO ACTION

Alyson, Sasha, ed. *You CAN Do Something About AIDS.* The Stop AIDS Project, 1988.

Helpful advice from a wide range of authors, from C. Everett Koop to Whoopi Goldberg.

Benjamin, Medea, and Freedman, Andrea. *Bridging the Global Gap: A Handbook to Linking Citizens of the First and Third Worlds.* Seven Locks, 1989.

A book to carry with you on your journey to the new internationalism; a practical passport to global citizenship. Treats human rights, fair trade, aid, travel with a purpose, and so on.

Brown, Lester R., et al. *State of the World: A Worldwatch Institute Report on Progress Toward a Sustainable Society*. W. W. Norton, 1991.

The best analysis of how to create a sustainable life-style for the entire planet. Especially good on questioning materialism. Published annually.

Buell, Becky. *Alternatives to the Peace Corps: Gaining Third World Experience*. Food First, 1988.

Ways to work in the world of development in programs not funded and controlled by the U.S. government.

Caplan, Ruth, and the Staff of Environmental Action. *Our Earth, Ourselves: The Action-oriented Guide to Help You Protect and Preserve Our Environment*. Bantam, 1990.

Action steps, portraits of people who've made a difference, and intelligent introductions to topics such as air pollution, global warming, and nuclear waste.

Council on Economic Priorities. *Shopping for a Better World*. Ballantine, 1991.

A quick and easy guide to socially responsible supermarket shopping.

Cowan, Jessica, ed. *Good Works: A Guide to Careers in Social Change*. Dembner, 1991.

A list of organizations working for social change and of volunteer and paid positions.

EarthWorks Group. *50 Simple Things You Can Do to Save the Earth*. EarthWorks Press, 1989.

EarthWorks Group. *50 Simple Things Kids Can Do to Save the Earth*. EarthWorks Press, 1990.

Suggestions for starting simple, with activities such as making sure your tires are properly inflated, substituting paper cups for Styrofoam, and snipping six-pack rings.

Erickson, Brad, ed. **Call to Action: Handbook for Peace, Justice, and Ecology.** Sierra Club, 1990.

Action steps, resources, and thoughtful reflection on economic justice, multi-cultural alliances, world hunger, pesticide addiction. First-rate contributors include Brian Willson on nonviolence and a preface by Jesse Jackson.

Five College Program in Peace and World Security Studies. **Guide to Careers, Internships, and Graduate Education in Peace Studies.** Hampshire College, 1990.

Just as the title says, a guide packed with information. Good bibliography, too.

George, Nelson, ed. **Stop the Violence: Overcoming Self-Destruction.** Pantheon, 1990.

A statement of taking responsibility for what is around us. Young rap stars talk about their efforts to stop violence at concerts. Includes startling photos, rap lyrics, and letters about black-on-black crime.

Gershen, Howard. **A Guide for Giving: 250 Charities and How They Use Your Money.** Pantheon, 1990.

A guide that gives purpose, size, income, amount spent on overhead, "little known facts" for charities. Leans toward mainstream (American Lung Association, Big Brothers) but includes Human Rights Watch, Christic Institute, Oxfam.

Head, Suzanne, and Heinzman, Robert, eds. **Lessons of the Rain-forest.** Sierra Club, 1990.

Essays on many aspects of the rain forest by major voices, such as Frances Moore Lappé (Food First), Randall Hayes (Rainforest Action Network), and Jason Clay (Cultural Survival).

Hollender, John. *How to Make the World a Better Place: A Beginner's Guide to Doing Good.* William Morrow, 1990.

A book full of good ideas for effecting positive social change. Lists of organizations, publications, and so on.

Kenyon, Thomas L., and Blau, Justine. *What You Can Do To Help the Homeless: Creative and Effective Contributions That Individuals, Families, and Businesses Can Make.* Simon & Schuster/Fireside, 1991.

Actions you may not have thought of, from special help for battered homeless women to getting involved in home sharing.

Lydenberg, Steven D., et al. *Rating America's Corporate Conscience: A Provocative Guide to the Companies Behind the Products You Buy Every Day.* Addison-Wesley, 1986.

The Washington Post says this book provides wheels on which the vehicles of creative protest move.

Morgan, Elizabeth, with Van Weigel and Eric DeBaufre. *Global Poverty and Personal Responsibility: Integrity Through Commitment.* Paulist Press, 1989.

An examination of the rarely considered dimension of moral responsibility of First Worlders.

Tree People. *The Simple Act of Planting a Tree: The Tree People Guide to Healing Your Neighborhood, Your City.* Tarcher, 1990.

A how-to book that includes a tree seed. You can do it!

Unitarian Universalist Service Committee. *The Busy Person's Guide to Social Action.* Unitarian Universalist Service Committee, 1986.

Information on running meetings, raising funds, dealing with the press, and so on. Written for Unitarian congregations, but its relevance is universal.

Withers, Leslie, and Peterson, Tom, eds. *Hunger Action Handbook: What You Can Do and How to Do It.* Seeds Magazine, 1987.

Simple, effective ways to address hunger in your community and around the world. How to start a soup kitchen, volunteer overseas, influence government policy, and so on.

COMPUTER CONFERENCE

PeaceNet
   Institute for Global Communications
   3228 Sacramento Street
   San Francisco, CA 94115
   415-923-0900

Partnerships for Change:
A Directory of Organizations

The following organizations are working for positive change in the world. Many of them can use volunteer help, most can use donations, and many supply information and support for action in local communities. The list is only a sampler; once you begin to investigate, you will find many more. Organizations mentioned in this book are also listed here.

AIDS

AIDS Action Committee
131 Clarendon Street
Boston, MA 02116
800-235-2331, 617-437-6200

Confidential AIDS information and referrals for the Boston area. Brochures on specific issues.

AIDS Coalition to Unleash Power—New York (ACT UP)
135 West 29th Street
New York, NY 10011
212-564-2437

AIDS Coalition to Unleash Power—San Francisco
2300 Market Street, Suite 68
San Francisco, CA 94114
415-563-0724

Activist-oriented coalition of people working for the rights of those affected by AIDS.

Chicago House and Social Service Agency, Inc.
P.O. Box 14728
Chicago, IL 60614
312-248-5200

"A special place to call home in a time of need." Provides housing and helps coordinate social services for people with AIDS.

The NAMES Project
2362 Market Street
San Francisco, CA 94114
415-863-5511

Creators and organizers of the AIDS Memorial quilt. The quilt has over 14,000 panels, but it's still possible to add another to honor a loved one. Write or call for instructions.

National AIDS Network (NAN)
203 M Street, NW, Suite 800
Washington, DC 20036
202-293-2437

Source of technical assistance, referral services, and grants to community-based AIDS organizations, hospitals, and educational facilities.

National Association of People with AIDS
2025 I Street, NW, Suite 1118
Washington, DC 20006
202-429-2856

An association of local organizations by and for people with AIDS.
Provides information and referrals, advocates for rights.

U.S. Department of Health and Human Services Hotline
800-342-2437

A source of information and names of organizations in your area.

ALTERNATIVE TRADE
ORGANIZATIONS

Equal Exchange
101 Tosca Drive
Stoughton, MA 02072
617-344-7227

A food importer trading directly with small-scale farmers in Nicaragua, Peru, and Mexico.

Friends of the Third World, Inc.
611 West Wayne Street
Fort Wayne, IN 46802-2125
219-422-1650

A strong supporter of alternative trade. Helps other groups start their own stores; publishes catalog of books, crafts, and food (wholesale and retail).

Pueblo to People
P.O. Box 2545
Houston, TX 77252-2545
713-523-1197

Publisher of a full-color catalog. Supports Latin American cooperatives that not only need income but are working for social impact.

THE ENVIRONMENT

Citizen's Clearinghouse for Hazardous Wastes
P.O. Box 926
Arlington, VA 22216
703-276-7070

National environmental organization started and led by grassroots activists (Love Canal). Provides information on toxic waste problems.

Council for Responsible Genetics
186 South Street, 4th Floor
Boston, MA 02111
617-423-0650

An information source that helps organize state conferences on biotechnology and publishes *GeneWatch*.

Creating Our Future
High School Environmental Action
398 South Ferndale
Mill Valley, CA 94941
415-381-6744

High school students working to save the rain forests.

Earth Island Institute
300 Broadway, Suite 28
San Francisco, CA 94133
415-788-3666

Sponsor, supporter, and coordinator of projects ranging from Japan Environmental Exchange to the Rainforest Health Alliance. Publishes *Earth Island Journal*, with "What You Can Do" ideas.

Greenpeace USA
1436 U Street, NW
Washington, DC 20009
202-462-1177

An action group that attends to a wide range of environmental concerns, from whales and clean air to toxic waste and global warming.

Mothers and Others for a Livable Planet
Natural Resources Defense Council
40 West Twentieth Street
New York, NY 10011
212-727-2700

A source of information on how families can work for solutions to environmental problems. Publishes the quarterly newsletter *tlc*.

Natural Resources Defense Council (NRDC)
40 West Twentieth Street
New York, NY 10168
212-949-0049

A center that combines legal action, citizen education, and scientific research to protect the environment.

Rainforest Action Network
301 Broadway, Suite A
San Francisco, CA 94133
415-398-4404

A network that works nationally and internationally to protect the world's rain forests. Publishes fact sheets, *Action Alert,* and *World Rainforest Report.*

Sierra Club
730 Polk Street
San Francisco, CA 94109
415-776-2211

A broad-based 100-year-old group that plans outings, sponsors educational campaigns, and is active in environmental advocacy. Many publications.

HUNGER AND HOMELESSNESS

Bread for the World
802 Rhode Island Avenue, NE
Washington, DC 20018
202-269-0200

A Christian advocacy group that organizes citizens to lobby Congress for sustainable, environmentally sound, grass-roots-based development abroad. Also addresses causes of hunger in the United States.

Community for Creative Non-Violence
425 Second Street, NW
Washington, DC 20001-2037
202-393-4409

A provider of direct service to the homeless, public education, and political activism. Mitch Snyder's legacy.

Daily Bread
2447 Prince St.
Oakland, CA 94705
415-848-3522

A volunteer food distribution network in Berkeley/Oakland. Provides information on creating such networks, starting garden projects, and so on.

Greyston Family Inn
114 Woodworth Avenue
Yonkers, NY 10701
914-375-1510

A source of permanent housing and support services for the reintegration of homeless families in their old neighborhoods. Provides job training through the Greyston Bakery.

Hunger Hotline
11 Beacon Street
Boston, MA 02108
617-523-7010

A source of information on where to get fed in the Boston area.

Institute for Food and Development Policy
(Food First)
145 Ninth Street
San Francisco, CA 94103
415-864-8555

A research and education center on political and economic causes of hunger.

The Learning Tree
98 Wellington Street
Springfield, MA 01109
413-733-7452

An alternative learning environment for inner-city youth that also provides meals and housing.

National Coalition for the Homeless
1621 Connecticut Avenue, NW, Suite 400
Washington, DC 20009
202-265-2371

An advocacy group involved in research, education, legislative advocacy, and litigation.

PEACE WORK

Children of War
85 South Oxford Street
Brooklyn, NY 11217
718-858-6882

An international youth leadership training program. Builds partnerships between young people from war zones and U.S. teenagers.

Equal Rights Congress
4705 South Main Street
Los Angeles, CA 90037
213-233-3715

With thirty-seven affiliates nationwide, a group that helps community-based organizations of color address issues related to peace and racial and economic equality.

Jobs with Peace National Network
76 Summer Street
Boston, MA 02110
617-338-5783

A network that educates and organizes to convert the economy from military to peace supporting.

The Listening Project
Rural Southern Voice for Peace
1898 Hannah Branch Road
Burnsville, NC 28714
704-675-5933

An empowerment process that trains activists in listening and better communication. Provides training sessions and publishes a manual.

Movement for a New Society
c/o Greg Bates
P.O. Box 1922
Cambridge, MA 02138
617-926-5560

A supplier of information for developing study circles.

National Association for Mediation in Education (NAME)
425 Amity Street
Amherst, MA 01002
413-253-5096

A good source for information about conflict resolution in schools; maintains a directory of active programs.

1% for Peace
P.O. Box 658 Ithaca, NY 14851
607-273-1919

A nonprofit, nonpartisan campaign devoted to moving the United States toward peace in positive ways. Included in their vision is a legislative agenda to redirect at least 1 percent of the Department of Defense budget to constructive, people-to-people programs for peace.

Peace Development Fund
44 North Prospect Street
P.O. Box 270
Amherst, MA 01004
413-256-8306

A supporter of locally based peace and social justice activities throughout the United States.

20/20 Vision
30 Cottage Street
Amherst, MA 01002
413-549-4555

A coordinator of local projects in which people give twenty minutes a month "to create a more secure world."

STUDY/WORK TOURS AND ALTERNATIVE TRAVEL

American Friends Service Committee
1501 Cherry Street
Philadelphia, PA 19102-1479
215-241-7295

A cosponsor of summer community service projects with Mexican and other Latin American organizations. Construction, gardening, child care, and arts and crafts projects for volunteers aged eighteen to twenty-six. Spanish fluency essential. There is a fee, and you are responsible for your own travel expenses.

Center for Global Education
Augsburg College
731 Twenty-first Avenue, South
Minneapolis, MN 55454
612-330-1159

A provider of travel seminars focusing on social justice concerns in Central America, Mexico, the Philippines, the Middle East, and southern Africa. Also offers an undergraduate academic program in Cuernavaca, Mexico.

Earthwatch
P.O. Box 403
Watertown, MA 02272
617-926-8200

An organization through which volunteers work with scientists and scholars on research expeditions in thirty-seven countries.

Food First Reality Tours
145 Ninth Street
San Francisco, CA 94103
415-864-8555

An organizer of study tours to the Third World with an emphasis on food and agriculture.

Habitat for Humanity
121 Habitat Street
Americus, GA 31709
912-924-6935

A group that places volunteers on stipends for three-year periods of construction and management in Asia, Latin America, Africa, and the Pacific Islands. Also short-term projects in North America and Mexico.

Institute for International Cooperation and Development
P.O. Box 103
Williamstown, MA 01267
413-458-9828

An organizer of a nine-month travel/study course in Central America and Asia. Also eleven- and twelve-month solidarity work courses in Mozambique (reforestation), Angola (education), and Nicaragua (construction).

Marazul Tours, Inc.
250 West Fifty-seventh Street, Suite 1311
New York, NY 10107
212-586-3847

An organizer of study tours to Cuba, Guatemala, Haiti, Mexico, Nicaragua, and Puerto Rico.

Peace Brigades International–USA
Woolman Hill
Keets Road
Deerfield, MA 01342
413-773-9738

A provider of nonviolent, nonpartisan peace teams in situations of violent conflict around the world (Sri Lanka, El Salvador, Guatemala, and so on).

Sister Cities Training
c/o Jobs with Peace
76 Summer Street
Boston, MA 02110
617-338-5783

A group that brings together local organizers to share information and technical assistance.

Veterans-Vietnam Restoration Project
716 Locust Street, P.O. Box 369
Garberville, CA 94440
707-923-3357

A group that sends teams to Vietnam to work on construction projects, build medical clinics, reconstruct orphanages, and restore relations.

THIRD WORLD SOLIDARITY/ HUMAN RIGHTS

American Committee on Africa
198 Broadway
New York, NY 10038
212-962-1210

A distributor of information on apartheid and U.S. involvement in it. Also sets up sister cities.

American Friends Service Committee
1501 Cherry Street
Philadelphia, PA 19102-1479
215-241-7169

A national and international Quaker organization "putting the power of love to work on behalf of those who need it most: the poor, the hungry, the hopeless victims of violence, discrimination, and injustice."

Amnesty International
322 Eighth Avenue
New York, NY 10001
212-807-8400

An organizational human rights organization that focuses on the release of prisoners of conscience. Individuals and local groups in many areas write letters and do other advocacy work.

Christic Institute
1324 North Capitol Street, NW
Washington, DC 20002
202-797-8106

An interfaith nonprofit center for law and national policy in the public interest. Concerned with human rights, social justice, and personal freedom at home and abroad.

Cultural Survival
11 Divinity Avenue
Cambridge, MA 02138
617-495-2562

A supporter of projects designed to help indigenous people survive.

GATT-Fly
Ecumenical Coalition for Economic Justice
11 Madison Avenue
Toronto, Ontario M5R 2S2
Canada
416-921-4615

The best source for information on the debt crisis.

International Development Exchange (IDEX)
777 Valencia Street
San Francisco, CA 94110
415-621-1494

A supporter of small-scale community development projects abroad. Links communities in educational partnerships with U.S. individuals, schools, and organizations.

International Indian Treaty Council
710 Clayton Street, No. 1
San Francisco, CA 94117
415-566-0251

An indigenous support organization; the international arm of the American Indian Movement (AIM). Can refer to local organizations in support of the rights of indigenous people.

Network in Solidarity with the People of Guatemala (NISGUA)
1314 Fourteenth Street, NW
Washington, DC 20005
202-483-0050

A group whose work includes a rapid response network for human rights violations, delegations to Guatemala, support for popular movement, a campaign against U.S. military aid, a project to improve Guatemala media coverage, and so on.

Oxfam America
115 Broadway
Boston, MA 02116
617-482-1211

A funder of self-help development and disaster relief in poor countries. Sponsors annual Fast for a World Harvest, which encourages
participation by communities throughout North America.

Palestine Solidarity Committee
P.O. Box 94762
San Francisco, CA 94127
415-861-1552

A group that works for Palestinian rights in the United States
through public education.

Seva Foundation
Dept. C
108 Spring Lake Drive
Chelsea, MI 48118-9701
313-475-1351

8 North San Pedro Road
San Rafael, CA 94903
415-492-1829

An international development organization, working on blindness
in Nepal and India and grass-roots empowerment in Guatemala.
In the United States, works with Native Americans and sponsors
retreats and conferences encouraging compassion in action.

World Neighbors
5116 North Portland Avenue
Oklahoma City, OK 73112
405-946-3333

A people-to-people organization working to eliminate hunger, disease, and poverty. Particularly interested in women in development.

VOLUNTEERING — GENERAL

City Year
11 Stillings Street
Boston, MA 02210
617-451-0699

An "urban peace corps" that engages volunteers aged seventeen to twenty-two for one year of service in inner-city Boston. Projects include urban gardens, day care, tutoring, violence prevention, food banks, and senior care. Also sponsors "City Year for a Day," engaging many people for one day of inner-city service.

Literacy Volunteers of America
5795 Widewaters Parkway
Syracuse, NY 13214-1846
315-445-8000

An organization that includes 400 programs in forty-two states, providing tutoring in reading and English as a second language.

National VOLUNTEER Center
1111 North Nineteenth Street, Suite 500
Arlington, VA 22209
703-276-0542

A group that works to mobilize volunteers and help organizations that use volunteers. Assists in developing local volunteer centers and corporate volunteer programs.

About the Authors

RAM DASS (a.k.a. Richard Alpert) has a Ph.D. from Stanford University and has taught at Stanford, the University of California, and Harvard University. In the early sixties he researched the use of psychedelic chemicals for behavior change with his colleague Timothy Leary. In the late sixties he met his guru, Neem Karoli Baba, in India and was renamed Ram Dass (Servant of God) and instructed to serve and feed people. Since that time Ram Dass has done volunteer work with the dying, prisoners, teenagers, people with AIDS, the homeless, ecological groups, and, through the Seva Foundation, which he helped to form, Guatemalan refugees and the blind in India and Nepal. He earns his living through lecturing and writing. The most recent of his books is *How Can I Help?* coauthored with Paul Gorman.

MIRABAI BUSH was educated at Duquesne University, Georgetown University, and the State University of New York at Buffalo. In the last year of her Ph.D. studies in literature, she left the university to travel through Europe and the Middle East to Asia. In India, she studied in a Buddhist monastery and met Neem Karoli Baba, who became a major influence in her life. In 1972, as part of the movement for more humane hospital birthing, she delivered her son at home on a farm. She is a cofounder and was director of Illuminations, Inc., a gift design and distribution company committed to "right livelihood." She has taught—often with Ram Dass—at the State University of New York, Naropa Institute, Lama Foundation, Omega Institute, and Interface. Her most recent work has been in grass-roots village development in Guatemala for the Seva Foundation, for which she has also served as chairperson, treasurer, and director of publications. She lives in western Massachusetts with her companion, E. J. Lynch, and her son, Owen.

OTHER BELL TOWER BOOKS

pure sound
e bell
mons us into
resent moment.
timeless ring
uth
pressed in
y different voices,
one magnifying
illuminating
sacred.
clarity of its song
nates within us
calls us away
n those things
ch often
ract us—
t which was,
t which might be—
That Which Is.

BEING HOME
A Book of Meditations
by Gunilla Norris
Photographs by Greta D. Sibley

An exquisite modern book of hours, a celebration
of mindfulness in everyday activities.
Hardcover 0-517-58159-0

NOURISHING WISDOM
A New Understanding of Eating
by Marc David

A practical way out of dietary confusion,
a book that reveals how our attitude to food
reflects our attitude to life.
Hardcover 0-517-57636-8

SANCTUARIES
A Guide to Lodgings in Monasteries, Abbeys,
and Retreats of the United States: The Northeast
by Jack and Marcia Kelly

The first in a series of regional guides for those
in search of spiritual renewal and a little peace.
Softcover 0-517-57727-5

GRACE UNFOLDING
Psychotherapy in the Spirit of the Tao-te ching
by Greg Johanson and Ron Kurtz

The interaction of client and therapist illuminated
through the gentle power and wisdom of Lao Tzu's
ancient Chinese classic.
Hardcover 0-517-58449-2

SELF-RELIANCE
The Wisdom of Ralph Waldo Emerson as Inspiration
for Daily Living

Selected and with an introduction by Richard Whelan
A distillation of Emerson's essential spiritual
writings for contemporary readers.
Softcover 0-517-58512-X

• • •

If, after reading this book, you would like to learn more about Seva or help in its work, you may write to the Seva Foundation, Dept. H, 108 Spring Lake Drive, Chelsea, MI 48118.

• • •